*Poverty
and Discrimination*

STUDIES IN SOCIAL ECONOMICS

Poverty
and Discrimination

Lester C. Thurow

THE BROOKINGS INSTITUTION
Washington, D.C.

© 1969 by

THE BROOKINGS INSTITUTION
1775 Massachusetts Avenue, N.W.
Washington, D.C. 20036

Second printing July 1970
Third printing February 1973
Fourth printing February 1975

ISBN 0-8157-8444-9
Library of Congress Catalog Card Number 69-18825

Foreword

In recent years the war on poverty and the attack on racial discrimination have been among the nation's most pressing domestic issues. Passage of the Economic Opportunity Act and of civil rights legislation has demonstrated that Americans do not regard poverty and discrimination as ineradicable, but efforts made to eradicate them have so far done little to improve the economic status of the most needy. Education and job training programs have been the principal instruments relied upon to overcome poverty. Although such programs may have promise for whites, their potential for blacks is greatly reduced by the persistence of discrimination. If there is to be real achievement, research must be directed toward a better understanding of the causes of, and the difference between, poverty as blacks know it and poverty as whites know it.

In this study Lester C. Thurow defines poverty and discrimination as problems of the distribution of income and evaluates the effectiveness of various methods of altering that distribution. After applying econometric techniques to an investigation of the factors involved, he finds that such general measures as creating tight labor markets, accelerating the rate of growth, and promoting labor mobility will not help blacks to the same extent as whites unless discrimination can be overcome. He examines how discrimination exacerbates for blacks all the other causes of poverty and concludes that specific programs to eliminate it must be devised.

Mr. Thurow is a member of the economics and management faculties at the Massachusetts Institute of Technology. The study,

vii

which was undertaken when he was a member of the economics faculty of Harvard University, was awarded the David A. Wells Prize for 1967–68 by that institution.

The research for several of the chapters was performed under a contract with the Office of Economic Opportunity, and was based in part on data collected by the Equal Employment Opportunity Commission, under section 709(c) of the Civil Rights Act of 1964, in cooperation with the Office of Federal Contract Compliance of the United States Department of Labor.

The author acknowledges with gratitude the constructive comments of the Brookings reading committee: Margaret S. Gordon, Albert Rees, and Harold W. Watts. The book does not reflect many of their views, but it is better for their efforts. He is also grateful to Gretchen Pfuetze for her excellent research assistance, without which the study would never have been completed. Evelyn P. Fisher carefully checked the statistical material for consistency and accuracy. The manuscript was edited by Frances M. Shattuck and the index was prepared by Florence Robinson.

Acknowledgment should also be made for the use of material published earlier, as follows: parts of Chapter 3 appeared in the *Quarterly Journal of Economics;* of Chapter 5 and Appendix G, in *Federal Programs for the Development of Human Resources* (papers prepared for a subcommittee of the U.S. Joint Economic Committee); and of Appendix A, in the *Review of Economics and Statistics.* Full citations appear in the footnotes where appropriate.

This volume is the fifth of the Brookings Studies in Social Economics, a special program of research and education on selected topics in the fields of health, education, social security, and welfare.

The views expressed here are those of the author and are not presented as the views of the Office of Economic Opportunity, the Equal Employment Opportunity Commission, or of the trustees, officers, or staff members of the Brookings Institution.

KERMIT GORDON
President

June 1969
Washington, D.C.

Contents

CHAPTER I

The Twin Problems

During the 1960s two social goals have become matters of national concern: the elimination of poverty, and the achievement of equal status for Negro and white citizens. The war on poverty is directed toward the first goal, civil rights legislation and programs to aid urban ghettos toward the second. These goals were once viewed as separable, but society is increasingly recognizing the interrelations between them.

To eliminate poverty, its causes must be discovered and altered. This book focuses on the causes of poverty, but it pays particular attention to the differences between the causes for whites and blacks. To what extent are the causes similar? To what extent are they distinct? Are there qualitative differences or are the differences merely quantitative? Will a program designed to eliminate white poverty also eliminate black poverty?

Both qualitative and quantitative investigations of poverty reveal that racial discrimination is an important factor. Much of the poverty suffered by blacks can be ascribed to discrimination in one of its many forms. Thus, programs designed to eliminate white poverty will not eliminate black poverty. Nor will the elimination of racial discrimination solve the problem of poverty. Discrimination and poverty are as intertwined as Siamese twins; they need two policies, one to fight the causes of poverty and another to reduce discrimination.

To reduce discrimination, the practices of discrimination must be examined. Who gains, and who loses? What are the essential means that allow one group to discriminate against another? Can government policies alter any of these methods? Or is the problem solely one of changing white attitudes? Answers to these questions are as essential to winning the war on poverty as they are to a successful solution of the war on discrimination.

Discrimination

Racial discrimination exists whenever race is a factor in predicting the opportunities open to an individual. Eliminating discrimination means that each racial group in the population has an equal chance to make its preferences felt and to determine its life style. Individual lives may be very different, but the distribution of opportunities should be identical for different races.

The impact of discrimination, however, would not end if individuals merely stopped discriminating. Restricting opportunities at one point in time has an important effect on later opportunities. Depriving a man of an equal education means that he has less education for the rest of his life and that his children are raised in a family with less education. In the broadest sense, eliminating discrimination involves eliminating the present effects of past inequities. Some of the effects are not reversible, but alternative compensation, such as greater job training, could be designed to reduce some of the inequity.

The interrelations between various facets of discrimination necessitate broad antidiscriminatory programs. Blacks have little political power because they have little economic power, but they also have little economic power because they have little political power. Lack of political and economic power may explain poor schooling, but low education levels reinforce that lack. In a world of vicious circles, efforts can be made to break the circle at its weakest link or to attack all links simultaneously. A strategy should be followed which will yield the greatest reduction in discrimination at the least cost, but finding such a strategy is difficult. No analytic model can really split a circle into separate links. Each link is too dependent on the others to be examined separately.

Such interrelationships mean that coordinated attacks must be made. Without economic advances, political gains will be limited, and vice versa. Logically, economic equality can be achieved without political equality, and occasionally this happens. The Chinese in Southeast Asia have economic equality or supremacy while suffering from political discrimination. However, when a group starts from a position of economic, political, and educational inferiority, such an anomaly is not likely to occur. A white political power structure could force changes on society that would eliminate economic discrimination, but realistically this will not happen. Black political power must grow with economic power. The full development of either depends on the other.

The economic link in the vicious circle of discrimination is the focus of interest here, but it must be realized that success on the economic front is limited by what is won in the political field. Improving economic opportunities is important, however, since economic resources allow control over those goods which money can buy. Economic opportunities do not guarantee political or cultural opportunities, but they are necessary conditions.

Differences between the income distributions for whites and blacks provide a natural measure of the extent of economic discrimination. If the distributions are identical, both consumption and production opportunities are identical; discrimination does not exist. Insofar as Negroes are concentrated at the lower end of the distribution, they are victims of economic discrimination.[1]

Programs to eliminate economic discrimination may take many forms: improvements in education, open housing, head start programs, fair employment laws, job training programs, guaranteed jobs, direct income redistribution, or any of a large number of other instruments. Although these programs may have impacts on other types of discrimination, their effect on economic discrimination is measured in terms of their success or failure in altering the differences in the real income distributions for whites and Negroes.

Poverty

The war on poverty is also designed to alter the distribution of income by raising everyone above the poverty line. The 22 million

[1] Since this book is focused primarily on poverty, discrimination is dealt with only as an interrelated factor. There is no attempt to treat its impact on Negroes with incomes in the middle and upper levels.

persons who were in poverty in 1968, white and black, are to be moved to higher income levels. The war on poverty is wider than the war on discrimination since 68 percent of the poor persons are white,[2] but it is also narrower since it is not designed to affect incomes above the poverty line. Realistically, however, it is extremely unlikely to leave those incomes unaffected. It is an attack on poverty, but it has obvious implications for the comparative distributions of white and Negro incomes. Currently the major effort to raise Negro incomes is buried in the war on poverty.

In 1967, 10.1 million families and unrelated individuals were officially classified as poor (Table 1-1). Poverty can be defined by absolute standards of living or by the desired shape of the income distribution. The official definition ($3,335 for an urban family of four in 1967) is an absolute definition;[3] defining the poverty line as 50 percent of the median income is a relative one. Absolute definitions are acceptable for short periods of time and for programmatic purposes, but not for the long run. Since poverty lines are based on relative judgments about acceptable minimum standards of living, they undoubtedly rise with rising income levels. If a poverty line had been set in 1947, it would not have been set at the levels chosen in the 1960s.

Essentially, the problems of poverty and discrimination are not controversies about absolute standards of living, but about relative incomes and the shape of the American income distribution. How much income inequality does America wish to tolerate? How shall income inequalities be distributed across races? These are the fundamental long-run questions.

This study attempts to isolate and quantify the factors which determine the shape of income distribution and changes in it, but the emphasis is on those factors which affect the bottom of the scale. The analysis is on a strategic and not a tactical level. The focus is on the causes of poverty, the means by which economic discrimination is practiced, and on the essential conditions for eliminating poverty and discrimination—not on the efficiency of 1968 programs used in the war on poverty.

[2] *Economic Report of the President, January 1969,* p. 151; U.S. Bureau of the Census, *Current Population Reports,* Series P-60, No. 55, "Family Income Advances, Poverty Reduced in 1967" (1968), p. 2.

[3] U.S. Bureau of the Census, "Family Income Advances," p. 2.

TABLE I-I

Incidence of Poverty among Families and Unrelated Individuals,
by Age, Color, and Sex, 1967[a]

Characteristic	Number of poor families and unrelated individuals[b] (millions)	Incidence of poverty[c] (percentage)
Total	10.1	16
Aged[d]	3.8	36
White	3.3	34
Male	1.2	22
Female	2.1	50
Nonwhite	0.5	58
Male	0.2	49
Female	0.2	68
Nonaged[e]	6.3	12
White	4.4	9
Male	2.5	6
Female	2.0	27
Nonwhite	1.9	28
Male	0.9	22
Female	1.0	54

Source: U.S. Bureau of the Census, *Current Population Reports*, Series P-60, No. 55, "Family Income Advances, Poverty Reduced in 1967" (1968), p. 7. Figures are rounded and will not necessarily add to totals.

a. Poverty is defined according to the Social Security Administration's poverty-income standard, which takes into account family size, composition, and place of residence. Poverty-income lines are adjusted for price changes.

b. A family is defined as two or more related persons residing together. An unrelated individual is a person aged fourteen years or over who is not living with relatives; he may be a one-person household by himself or be part of a household.

c. Poor families and unrelated individuals as a percentage of the total number of families and unrelated individuals in the category.

d. All families headed by a person aged sixty-five or over and all unrelated individuals aged sixty-five or over.

e. All families headed by a person under age sixty-five and all unrelated individuals under age sixty-five.

Method Used

This book applies econometric techniques to the problems of poverty and discrimination. Although based on past data, it is not a definitive summary of the causes of poverty and discrimination in society in the late 1960s. The use of econometric techniques to study poverty and discrimination is only beginning. Experience with econometric forecasting models of the entire economy shows that models and equations must go through extensive refining before they can be used with great confidence, and they will never reach the point where they cannot be improved. There is no reason to assume that models analyzing the distribution of income will follow a different historical pattern. But there is no reason to postpone work on the problem.

Econometric techniques possess several merits. The mathematical framework of econometrics requires that assumptions concerning causation and the interrelationships between different variables be made explicit and be clearly labeled. If the assumptions are false or questionable, it will be easy to criticize them, but this is an advantage rather than a disadvantage. More accurate structures of causation can be developed only if current assumptions are clearly expressed.

In the process of developing econometric models, economic theory must be continually developed and refined. This process is seen in the development of models of the American economy; investment theory needs to be reexamined in order to estimate investment functions. Such reformulations of theory are even more important in the study of income distribution, where theory is much less developed than in macroeconomics. There has been some theoretical work on the distribution of income between capital and labor, but practically none on distribution among persons or families, and that little is much too loosely formulated to be tested with econometric equations.

For developing public policies to alter the distribution of income, quantitative as well as qualitative relationships must be found. Society may wish to alter the distribution, but it wishes to use the most efficient instrument possible. That choice requires quantitative knowledge about the factors that affect distribution. It is widely agreed that education affects incomes. The question is how much, and whose income? It is agreed that discrimination affects the distribution. Again, how much, and whose income? Econometric techniques can provide estimates of quantitative impacts, which can be relevant to policy makers.

Econometric techniques also provide statistical tests of the observed relationships. Is the relationship significant or insignificant? Should the hypothesized structure of causation be accepted or rejected? The methods developed for answering these questions are not infallible, but they are better than ignoring the questions.

At the same time, econometric techniques do have limitations. Results are presented in precise numerical forms, but they are subject to error and may seem more accurate than they are. Statistical estimates of the errors involved are always presented and should be kept in mind when evaluating the results.

In addition, the desire for precise mathematical representation may lead to oversimplification at the expense of reality. Precise specification makes assumptions explicit, but it also leads to simplification. Factors that are important but difficult to quantify may be ignored. The absence or limitation of the data leads to compromises between what is desired and what is possible.

Furthermore, models may be incorrectly specified. Explanatory factors may be incorrectly ignored or included. Causation may not work in the manner set out in the equations, creating misleading results. Variables may be statistically correlated with each other without being causally related. The search for good correlations may come to dominate economic theory and common sense.

Ultimately every equation and every model must be examined in the light of its statistical properties, economic theory, and any other information that seems relevant. The reader is urged to carry his critical judgment with him through the book and to retain a skeptical frame of mind. The results are not meant to be accepted in toto.

Many of the problems and limitations of particular models and equations are mentioned in the text. Other possible objections are discussed in critical appendixes, which are designed to aid in evaluating the results. Some of the problems cannot be overcome without more data; others will require more extensive theoretical and empirical work.

Scope of the Book

Chapter 2 of this volume pictures the extent of poverty and discrimination in America over the years 1929–67. Both the shapes and movements of the income distributions for whites and Negroes are closely examined. Chapter 3 is an overall view of the causes of poverty. General causal factors are introduced and then discussed in detail in the next five chapters. There is a detailed investigation of the role of resource utilization, human capital, mar-

ket imperfections, racial discrimination, and an inability to partic-
ipate in the productive economy.

In each chapter, except Chapter 7, Negroes and whites are
treated separately in order to investigate qualitative and quantitative differences in the causes of their poverty. Chapter 7 investigates directly the theory and practice of discrimination and attempts to quantify further some of the effects discussed in earlier
chapters. Chapter 8 deals with several special problems; a final chapter summarizes the findings.

CHAPTER II

Income as Measurement

Insofar as whites are concentrated in high income classes and Negroes in low, Negroes suffer from economic discrimination.[1] A measure of that discrimination is provided by the difference in their income distributions. Wide individual income differences may exist, but there should be no systematic differences between the proportions of each group in various income classes. An individual's probability of living in poverty or affluence would not depend on his race in a world without racial discrimination.

Differences between the income distributions of whites and Negroes provide a dynamic measure of discrimination as well as a static one. The dynamic measure is provided by changes in the differences: if the differences are narrowing, discrimination is declining; if they are widening, discrimination is increasing. The pace at which the differences are changing without specific government programs is an important factor in determining the magnitude of such programs that may be necessary to eliminate discrimination by a specific future date. If the differences are rapidly disappearing, special government programs may be unnecessary; if not, programs will be needed.

The distribution of income is important in the war on poverty

[1] This assumes that Negro and white preferences respecting work and leisure would be identical in the absence of present and past discrimination and that there are no other significant economic differences between whites and blacks that would not end when discrimination ends. Different ethnic groups with the same incomes can suffer from discrimination if they have different preferences. For this study blacks are assumed to have the same set of preferences concerning economic affairs as whites.

9

also. Here the goal is some explicit change at the bottom of the distribution. Before the goal can be specified, however, poverty must be clearly defined. Different definitions of poverty imply different distributions of income. Successfully raising all families to a $3,335 poverty line will not produce the same income distribution as raising every family to 50 percent of the median family income. As with discrimination, the speed with which individuals are escaping from poverty without the aid of government programs is important in determining the magnitude of the programs necessary to eliminate poverty by a specific future date.

The Market System

In a market economy the income distribution plays a central role in the allocation of goods and services. Individual preferences determine market demands, but preferences are weighted by income before they are communicated to the market. If an individual has no income, his potential demand for goods and services has no effect on the market. He must have income with which to make his preferences felt. The income distribution, being a measure of the allocation of potential purchasing power, measures the weight given to individual preferences in making economic decisions.

The achievement of efficiency in a market system depends on the prior achievement of an optimum distribution of income. If income is distributed in accordance with society's preferences, individual preferences are properly weighted in the marketplace and the market can then efficiently adjust to an equitable set of demands. If income is not distributed in accordance with society's preferences, the market adjusts to an inequitable set of demands. Market signals do not express society's desires and the market system does not result in an acceptable distribution of goods and services.

A market system generates incomes in the process of producing and distributing goods and services. Individuals earn income by that production and distribution. Although a market system may efficiently handle the demands for goods and services flowing from society's desired income distribution, there is nothing in the system that automatically achieves the desired distribution. One of the continuing functions of government is to alter the market income distribution to that desired by society. Taxes, transfer payments, and direct expenditures, such as those on education and the war on poverty, are all tools used in the effort.

Achieving the desired income distribution does not settle all allocation questions. Many goods, such as police protection, are not usually provided by the market. The cost of such public goods still must be allocated. In addition, society may have more egalitarian ideas about the distribution of particular goods than it does about goods in general. There is nothing irrational in deciding that the distribution of medical care should be more equal than the distribution of cars or TV sets. Incomes might be distributed to achieve the desired distribution of cars and TV sets, but other nonmarket arrangements may be necessary to achieve society's desired distribution of medical care. Thus the distribution of income is not the only allocative decision which society must make, but it is certainly one of the most important.

Choosing a desired income distribution is ultimately a public value judgment made through the political process. Although the economist has neither special knowledge nor prerogatives in expressing his opinions about optimum income distributions, the choice cannot be divorced from other economic decisions. Incomes serve as both a source of potential purchasing power and a system of work incentives. The income distribution which is most equitable according to society's preferences may not produce the most work. Therefore, the distribution may affect the total amount to be distributed. As a result, society must consider the problem of economic growth when it considers the problem of desired income distribution.

As general income levels rise, however, there is no reason why the trade-off between additional output and a more equitable income distribution should remain constant. If additional income becomes less important as society grows richer, progressively less weight needs to be placed on the importance of monetary work incentives. In addition, different methods of redistributing income may have very different effects on work incentives. Some redistribution systems may discourage work effort; others may actually increase it.[2]

In most cases there is no a priori method of determining the qualitative effect of redistribution systems on work incentives. In no case is there an a priori method of determining the quantitative effect. In addition to income, a host of nonmonetary incentives and work constraints influence work effort. Promotions, demotions, praise, and economic power all provide alternative incentive systems. Assembly lines, bosses, and a standard working day all prevent individuals from altering their work effort. In many cases these other incentives and constraints dominate the effects of income on work effort. Thus empirical information must be gathered to determine the connection between work effort and income distribution before the importance of the connection can be determined.

Economists can delineate the connection between economic growth and the distribution of income and between work incentives and specific redistribution plans. If there are unavoidable conflicts between the income distribution and economic growth, however, society must reconcile the different goals. Society may choose an income distribution that does not provide maximum work incentives, one that does not provide the ideal distribution of purchasing power, or one that meets neither goal fully. Unfortunately no method exists to avoid such choices.

In a democracy, the factors that determine the desired distribution of income are as varied as the factors that influence individual preferences. All sorts of constraints might be placed on the acceptable shape of the income distribution. These constraints may be based on beliefs about absolute or relative minimum survival standards or about the proper distribution of economic power. Since economic and political power are related, a democratic form of government might demand constraints on the income distribution in order to achieve political equality. Social problems, such as those presented by low income minority groups, influence the shape of the desired distribution. Poverty that is concentrated among a

[2] Differences will occur depending on the strength of the income and substitution effects in different systems of redistribution.

racial minority might be more intolerable than poverty spread across the population. The stability of individual positions in the income distribution also plays an important role in social judgments. Society would probably tolerate a much more unequal income distribution if the same individuals, families, and social groups were not consistently at the top or bottom. Lifetime incomes as well as annual incomes are important in choosing a desired income distribution.

A Measure of Well-being

Ideally the distribution of welfare should be examined instead of the distribution of income. Theoretically such a measure could take into account differences in the utility derived from income by different individuals and the benefits received from nonmonetary items such as leisure. Thus it would provide a much more comprehensive measure of well-being than income. Unfortunately, welfare and utility are not quantifiable concepts. Income must be used as a surrogate which is assumed to approximate the distribution of welfare. If individual preferences for income and leisure differ widely, income is not a good proxy. Some uniformity of individual preferences is required.

Since income can be defined in many different ways, care must be taken in choosing the appropriate definition of it. When income is being used as a surrogate for general welfare, the most general and comprehensive income definition should be used. Ideally, wages, dividends, rents, capital gains (realized and unrealized), income in kind, and the annuity value of wealth should be included to allow a more comprehensive measure of the definition of potential purchasing power than that usually required for tax purposes. Incomes determined in this manner would then be adjusted for relative costs of living (urban-rural, North-South, and so forth). Unfortunately we do not come close to having a completely comprehensive measure of income. Many items have not been computed adequately, others are difficult to compute conceptually. In practice we must accept the use of income rather than welfare and the use of a less than perfect income measure.

The unit of aggregation as well as the income definition is important in selecting the desired income distribution. Is society interested in family or individual income? Family incomes are usually chosen, since families are the relevant spending units, but a choice still must be made between total family income and per capita family income. If all decisions were rationally made (including decisions about family size) and if individual welfare were not the ultimate social goal, only family income should be considered. Under this theory, if a family reduces its per capita income by having children, family welfare must increase or it would not have children. Since family decisions are not completely rational and deliberate and since individual welfare is an important social goal, society must be interested in per capita family income as well as total family income. This creates the knotty problem of determining economies of scale in family costs of living. Are there such economies for large families, and if so, what is their magnitude? These questions remain largely unanswered.

Income may be the best and central tool for investigating the distribution of welfare, but the problems mentioned indicate that it has some serious limitations. As a result, care must be taken not to exaggerate the significance of income as a measure of welfare. At best it is only a rough approximation of the distribution.

Distribution in the United States

In 1967 the median income for primary families and individuals was $7,094. Nineteen percent of the American population (37 million individuals) were living in households with less than $4,000, but 25 percent were living in households with incomes of over $12,000. Shifting the income distribution to a per capita income measure does not radically alter this picture. Large families are an important cause of low per capita family incomes, but—contrary to popular belief—the median family size rises as incomes rise. In 1967 the median family size rose from 2.44 persons for families with incomes under $1,000 to 3.84 persons for families with incomes in the $25,000–$50,000 range. As a result, the per capita income distribution is less disperse than the family income distribution. Thirteen percent of persons in families were living in households with per capita incomes of less than $1,000, while another 13 percent were living in households with per capita incomes of over $4,000. The median per capita family income was $2,456.[3]

Income data from the U.S. Bureau of the Census do not include information about the distribution of either capital gains or wealth.[4] Without some knowledge about the distribution of these two major items no social judgments can be made about a particular income distribution.

Data on unrealized capital gains are practically nonexistent. The limited data that are available on realized capital gains, however, indicate that they primarily affect high incomes. Realized capital gains account for less than 2 percent of the income of those with incomes under $10,000, but for those with incomes between $500,000 and $1,000,000 they account for more than 60 percent of income.[5] Unrealized capital gains might be slightly more important at the lower income ranges, but low income families lack large assets to produce capital gains.

There is very little information concerning wealth. Lampman states that the top 2 percent of American families hold 29 percent of personal equity;[6] Goldsmith reports that 40 percent of net worth is held by the top 10 percent of households.[7] Among fami-

[3] U.S. Bureau of the Census, *Current Population Reports*, Series P-60, No. 59, "Income in 1967 of Families in the United States" (1969), pp. 2, 39, 54. A primary family comprises the head of a household and all other persons in the household related to the head. If nobody in the household is related to the head, then the head himself constitutes a "primary individual." A household can contain only one primary family or primary individual.

[4] The census income figures include income from wages and salaries, income from self-employment, dividends, interest, net rental income, income from estates and trusts, public assistance or welfare payments, unemployment compensation, pensions, annuities, alimony, royalties, and any regular income from other sources, such as contributions from persons not living in the same household. Money received from the sale of property, withdrawal of bank deposits, borrowing, tax refunds, irregular gifts, and lump-sum inheritances or insurance payments are not counted as income.

[5] Richard Goode, *The Individual Income Tax* (Brookings Institution, 1964), p. 195.

[6] Robert J. Lampman, "Changes in the Share of Wealth Held by Top Wealth-Holders, 1922–1956," *Review of Economics and Statistics*, Vol. 41 (November 1959), p. 391.

[7] Goode, *Individual Income Tax*, p. 334. Based on Raymond W. Goldsmith, Dorothy S. Brady, and Horst Mendershausen, *A Study of Saving in the United States* (Princeton University Press, 1956), Vol. 3.

lies with incomes of less than $3,000, net assets amounted to only $2,760 at the end of 1962.[8] These limited assets would be quickly reduced to zero in attempts to rise above the poverty line, and if transformed into annuities would make little difference to the distribution of income.

As previously mentioned, the stability of individual positions in the income distribution, as well as the shape of it, is important in determining preferences about the desired distribution. Individual positions at the lower end seem to be relatively stable. Only 19 percent of the families with incomes of less than $3,000 in 1962 managed to move to higher income levels in 1963. Two-fifths of this number were able to move only into the next bracket ($3,000–$4,000).[9] Although there are some families with temporarily low incomes, most families are consistently at the bottom of the distribution.

All these factors mean that the standard income distributions are considerably more accurate as measures of welfare in the middle and bottom ranges than in the upper range. Although an income measure which ignores capital gains and wealth is not useful for many purposes, it provides a fairly good gauge of potential purchasing power at the lower end of the distribution.

The distributions of constant dollar personal income for 1929, 1947, and 1963 indicate the changes that have taken place in income distribution (see Figure 2-1). The distribution is not a bell-shaped curve that gradually moves from left to right. As income rises from low levels the distribution changes from a steeply falling straight line (note the 1947 nonwhite income distribution in Figure 2-2) to a bell-shaped distribution. As incomes continue to rise, the bell moves to the right but it also becomes flatter. Relative measures of income dispersions indicate that there was some movement to a more equal distribution before and during the Second World War, but that since then there has been no marked change.[10] What should be pointed out, however, is that the measures that indicate stability in the postwar period are all relative,

[8] *Economic Report of the President, January 1965,* p. 163.
[9] *Ibid.,* p. 164.
[10] See sources for Figure 2-2.

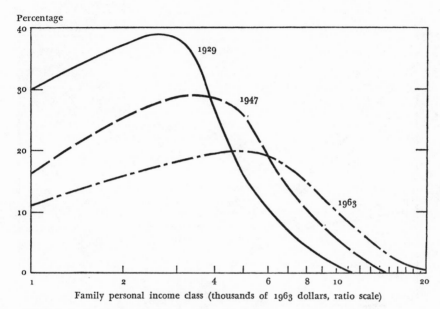

FIGURE 2-1

*Distribution of Personal Income of Families and Unrelated
Individuals, by Income Class, 1929, 1947, and 1963*

Family personal income class (thousands of 1963 dollars, ratio scale)

Source: *Survey of Current Business*, Vol. 44 (April 1964), Table 2, p. 4.

measuring the fraction of total income accruing to different frac-
tions of the total population. Consistency in these measures signi-
fies increasing absolute disparities. The top quartile may have
seven times as much income as the bottom quartile in both 1947
and 1967, but a 60 percent rise in average real incomes from 1947
to 1967 implies a large increase in the absolute income differences.
Thus both absolute and relative measures of dispersion are important in making social judgments about the desired income distribution. In the postwar period there has been no change in the relative dispersion across income classes, but the absolute differences
have widened. Between 1947 and 1967 the difference between the
median income levels for the top fifth and bottom fifth of the fami-

FIGURE 2-2

Distribution of Money Income of Families and Unrelated
Individuals, by Color, 1947 and 1965

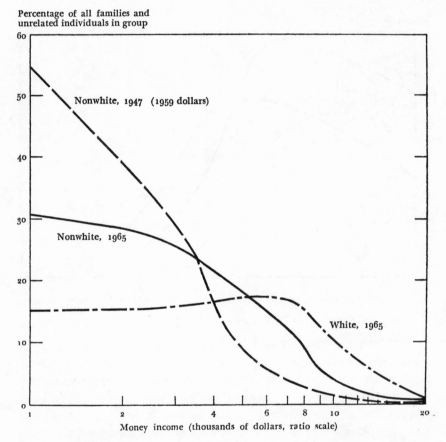

Percentage of all families and
unrelated individuals in group

Money income (thousands of dollars, ratio scale)

Sources: U.S. Bureau of the Census, *Trends in the Income of Families and Persons in the United States: 1947 to 1960*, Technical Paper No. 8 (1963), p. 188, and *Current Population Reports*, Series P-60, No. 51, "Income in 1965 of Families and Persons in the United States" (1967), p. 18.

lies increased by $5,770 (in constant 1967 dollars) in spite of the relative constancy in the share of total income received by each group.[11]

[11] Based on data in U.S. Bureau of the Census, "Income in 1967 of Families in the United States," p. 26.

Distribution as a Measure of Discrimination

The impact of economic discrimination can be seen in the difference in income distribution for whites and Negroes. In 1967 the median income of primary families and individuals was $4,187 for Negroes and $7,409 for whites. Although only 19 percent of the white households had incomes below $3,000, almost 37 percent of the Negro households fell into this category. At the upper end of the income distribution 31 percent of the white households had incomes over $10,000, but only 12 percent of the Negroes were similarly situated.[12]

Some insights into the movement of nonwhite incomes can be gained by comparing the 1965 nonwhite income distribution with other distributions for both whites and nonwhites (Figures 2-1 and 2-2). In 1965 the average (mean) nonwhite income per family and unattached individual was just slightly larger than the 1929 average income for both whites and nonwhites (in constant dollars).[13] Both the mean and the shape of the 1965 nonwhite distribution look more like the 1929 national than the 1965 white, but there are important differences. The 1965 nonwhite is slightly more disperse than the 1929 national. Both the 1929 national and the 1965 nonwhite show approximately 30 percent of the households with incomes of less than $2,000 and 6–7 percent with incomes above $10,000. Between $2,000 and $10,000, however, the 1965 nonwhite distribution is less concentrated than the 1929 national. In 1929, 54 percent of the families and unattached individuals had incomes between $2,000 and $6,000, but in 1965 only 45 percent of nonwhites were in that category. In 1929, 10 percent of the households were in the $6,000 to $10,000 range, but in 1965, 17 percent of the nonwhites were in it.

Job opportunities in the $6,000 to $10,000 income range were much more limited in 1929. Given the increasing number of opportunities for high income since created by the economy (in 1965

[12] *Ibid.*, p. 54.
[13] *Ibid.*, No. 51, "Income in 1965 of Families and Persons in the United States," p. 18, and *Survey of Current Business*, Vol. 44 (April 1964), p. 4.

over 30 percent of whites were in that bracket) and the increase in female workers in the labor force, the higher number of nonwhites is not surprising. Obviously some of them were able to take advantage of economic opportunities.

The changes that have occurred within the nonwhite distribution can be seen by comparing the 1965 and 1947 figures. In 1947 the distribution (in 1959 dollars) was a steeply falling line. In the following eighteen years it started to develop the familiar bell shape, although the bell is not as pronounced as that for whites. Based on historical observations of what has been happening to the distributions of white and nonwhite incomes, the two distributions seem to be evolving in the same general direction. The shapes of the distributions are not radically different when standardized for different average income levels, but the nonwhite population seems to be lagging some thirty years behind the white population.

Poverty Defined

As distributions of income demonstrate, there is no clearly defined group that can be called poor. No amount of research will discover a "poverty line" inherent in the income distribution itself. Perhaps this caveat should be kept in mind in all attempts to "discover" a poverty line.

Depending on usage and aims, there are many relevant definitions of poverty. There is no reason why the definitions should be the same for economic, sociological, or cultural poverty or why the same individuals should be identified under different definitions. There is also no reason why the same definition should be used for every program designed to help the poor. Perhaps eligibility requirements for income supplement programs should be radically different from those for programs to increase human capital or provide cultural enrichment.

Economic analysis should recognize that there is a poverty *band* rather than a poverty line. No one can logically define and defend any precise dollar figure as the poverty line or as equally valid for all uses. This would be true if there were no problems in defining and calculating a comprehensive income measure. Given the data inadequacies inherent in any income measure and the estimating errors that emerge whatever definition is selected, the search for a single poverty line is utopian at best. Instead of argument whether the poverty line for a family of four is $2,500 or $3,500, there should be recognition that there is a band over which definite poverty shades into economic sufficiency; this band might well be as wide as $1,000. For specific programs specific dollar figures must be established, just as the line between hot and cold must occasionally be drawn, but when the problem of poverty is under discussion, there is certainly no need to be restricted in this way.

Definitions of poverty can be constructed on four varied bases:

1. A fraction of the income distribution.

2. Explicit goals for the relative shape of income distribution.

3. Estimates of the minimum income level necessary to guarantee healthy survival.

4. Adequate standards of living as seen by the majority of the population.

The first two definitions both have the advantage of emphasizing that there are income distribution goals beyond those of merely setting minimum standards of living.

Under the first definition the bottom 15 percent of the income distribution could be impoverished regardless of actual income. In this sense poverty cannot be eliminated or reduced, but the income distribution can be narrowed by raising the bottom.

The second definition could classify as poor anyone below 50 percent of the median income. Elimination of poverty would come about through programs designed to bring the entire lower quartile up to the income of the second quartile.

The third possibility takes as key items the estimated costs of minimum amounts of shelter, clothing, and food. Such estimates place the poverty line at a very low level. The patterns of living at such an income level are radically different from the style of life led by the rest of the population (particularly the diets) and from that previously led by the poor themselves.

Under the fourth definition both absolute and relative individual preferences are important in locating the poverty line. In most

societies, these judgments will not demand radically different personal habits from those of the majority, but the poverty standards
will vary depending on the income levels of the country. Additionally, as the incomes of the majority rise, the poverty line will probably also rise. There are no statistics that can be called forth to justify a particular line, but this in no way invalidates the definition.
The lack of hard statistics merely emphasizes that individual value
judgments are central, change over time, and lack precision. They
cannot be made down to the last dollar. In the long run, the
fourth definition of poverty merges into the second. Long-run relative standards of living dominate short-run absolute standards.

All four approaches to defining poverty provide interesting insights and have some validity, but the definitions that have actually been adopted are based primarily on the fourth approach.
The vagueness of the poverty line suggested by it, however, has
frequently led to the use of calculations made according to the
third alternative. This often requires rather strained procedures.
Given the energy devoted to criticizing and defending the definition of poverty, it might have been wiser to admit that the definition is based on government judgments about individual preferences concerning the desired income distribution.

Three thousand dollars was established as the poverty line by
the Council of Economic Advisers (CEA) in its 1964 Annual Report. Later the official Social Security Administration-Office of
Economic Opportunity definition set the line at $3,130 for a fam-
ily of four in 1964.[14] Unfortunately, the programmatic necessity of
drawing a line at some explicit dollar amount seemed to give these
estimates a specious accuracy and to invite countless attacks on
their validity. They are easily criticized. The $3,000 figure was
meant to represent income for a family of four; but, due to the
lack of data, all families were originally used in counting the number in poverty. Objections were made that the figure did not allow
for family size, assets, or differences in costs of living.

The Social Security Administration definition eliminated some
of these problems and created others. The definition started by
pricing a Department of Agriculture low-cost food plan which did

[14] Mollie Orshansky, "Counting the Poor: Another Look at the Poverty Profile,"
Social Security Bulletin (January 1965), pp. 3–29.

not deviate radically from the average food habits of the population. On the assumptions that all expenditures were proportional to food expenditures and that total budgets were three times as large as food budgets (the national average for all income classes in 1955), poverty lines could be constructed for a variety of family sizes and types. The precise basket of food chosen, the assumption that all other expenditures are proportional to food expenditures, and the multiplier of three provoked easy quarrels. These quarrels, most of which attempted to substitute one speciously precise estimate for another, served only to dissipate energy that could have found other uses. Because the $3,130 definition (which was increased to $3,335 by 1967) is not a line but merely a shorthand way of describing a poverty band, its main value is evidence about individual preferences on the adequacy of the definition. However, since the political process has opted for this definition, it must be accepted for the time being as the social definition of poverty.

To make empirical studies of the factors which influence poverty, it is also necessary to use poverty lines rather than bands, but they should always be thought of as representing midpoints of poverty bands. Different poverty definitions are used in this book when they seem to add something to the analysis or when they correspond to the manner in which the basic data are organized. For many purposes the official Social Security Administration definition is preferable to that of the CEA, but much of the analysis is carried out using the CEA definition, since census data are usually not available to fit the official one.

Summary

Using the $3,000 poverty line for families and a $1,500 poverty line for unrelated individuals, poverty declined by about 0.8 percentage point per year (in constant 1967 dollars) for both groups between 1947 and 1967. In 1967, 12 percent of the families and 35 percent of the unrelated individuals were still poor.[15] If the rate of

[15] U.S. Bureau of the Census, "Income in 1967 of Families in the United States," p. 22.

decline of 0.8 percentage point per year continued after 1967, fifteen years would be necessary to eliminate poverty among families and forty-four years among unattached individuals. Since the poverty line rises as average incomes rise, the actual period will be even longer. Even if the rate of decline does not slow down and the definition of poverty is not changed (see Chapter 8), these time estimates are probably too long to be socially tolerated. If some plausible long-run definition of poverty, such as 50 percent of the median income, is used, there has been no progress in eliminating poverty. The proportion of all American families with incomes of less than one-half the median income for the country as a whole has remained constant at about one-fifth since 1947.[16]

The need for specific government programs to alter the income distribution is further confirmed by the lack of progress in eliminating discrimination. In the postwar period the median family income of nonwhites has been stable at 55 percent ($\pm$ 4 or 5 percent) of that of whites, with a slight upsurge occurring in 1966–67. On the basis of relative income measures, discrimination has changed little. Absolute measures, indeed, indicate a widening gap. In 1947 the difference between white and nonwhite median family incomes was $2,302 (in 1967 dollars). By 1967 the difference had expanded to $3,133.[17] The nonwhite income distribution seems to be following the same historical pattern as the white income distribution, but there is little evidence that the time lag between the two distributions is narrowing, the nonwhite remaining about thirty years behind the white.

In view of two decades of near stability in the relative shares of income received by different income classes and in the differences between white and nonwhite incomes, there is no reason to predict abrupt changes in the shape of the income distribution, the extent of discrimination, or the speed with which poverty is eliminated. The burden of proof is certainly on those who believe that changes in the economy will alter the nature of the income distribution. That distribution is actually a product of the under-

[16] U.S. Bureau of the Census, *Current Population Reports*, Series P-60, No. 54, "The Extent of Poverty in the United States: 1959 to 1966" (1968), p. 2.

[17] U.S. Bureau of the Census, "Income in 1967 of Families in the United States," pp. 22, 23.

lying distributions of human and physical capital, the level of productivity, the organization of the economic system, discrimination, and many other factors. Unless positive evidence can be found that these elements are going to change autonomously, there is no reason to think that the income distribution will suddenly start to take new directions.

Relative differences among income classes and races will probably remain fairly constant in the foreseeable future, and absolute measures of dispersion will increase. If the existing distributions are not satisfactory, positive measures must be taken to alter them. Neither the problem of discrimination nor the related problem of poverty will be solved automatically by continued economic growth.

CHAPTER III

The Causes of Poverty

A market system of economics generates incomes in the process of producing and distributing goods and services. Returns are given to those who own land and capital and to those who provide their labor services. In a study of poverty and discrimination, individual labor is the important source of income—the ownership of land and capital being relatively unimportant except at the highest income levels.

Theoretically labor income is determined by labor's marginal productivity. Workers are paid according to how much they contribute to marginal increases in output. If increasing the number of employed workers by one worker would increase output by $5,000, workers should be paid $5,000. Insofar as this is true in practice, higher earnings merely reflect a higher marginal productivity for labor. If an individual's income is too low, his productivity is too low. His income can be increased only if his productivity can be raised. To raise a laborer's productivity requires knowledge of the factors that lead to changes in his marginal product.

It is evident that the sources of growth of labor's marginal product are closely related to the sources of output growth. The quantitative importance of various sources of economic growth is still being discussed among economists,[1] but the sources being consid-

[1] The standard reference work is Edward F. Denison, *The Sources of Economic Growth in the United States and the Alternatives Before Us* (Committee for Economic Development, 1962).

ered would include the quantity of capital and labor, their quality (technical progress embodied in capital and labor), economies of scale, improvements in economic organization (disembodied technical progress), and increases in knowledge, all of which influence the marginal productivity of labor as well as the level of output. One method of studying these sources is to use an aggregate production function; this is done in the following section.

However, workers may not be paid according to their marginal productivities. In addition, many individuals are outside the productive economy. Reasons for their being totally or partially outside the labor force include age, family responsibilities, health, and job availabilities. Thus analysis of the income distribution must go beyond the factors which determine labor's marginal product and bring in others such as discrimination, age, market imperfections, and the adequacy of aggregate demand.

The causes of poverty are difficult to detect from descriptive classifications of the poor. There is a wide variety of possible explanations, which are so closely interrelated that it is difficult to distinguish their qualitative and quantitative importance. A method of determining their relative importance is to specify the relationships between poverty and possible causes in an econometric model, which provides a technique for quantifying the factors involved. This will be developed later in this chapter.

Labor's Marginal Product

An aggregate production function can be used to analyze the factors that determine the level of output.[2] If the same production function is, instead, differentiated with respect to labor, a mathematical expression is derived for the marginal productivity of labor (see Appendix A). The explanatory variables and parameters in the production function are identical with those in the marginal productivity equation. By inserting the parameters from the production

---

[2] An alternative approach is to assume that factors of production are paid their marginal products. Observed incomes can then be used to analyze the sources of growth. *Ibid.*

function and the data to which it was applied into the equation for the marginal productivity of labor, labor's marginal product can be estimated empirically. The great advantage of the procedure is that it does not require the assumption that workers are actually paid according to their marginal productivity.

If this approach is used with the production function described in Appendix A, labor's marginal product in the private American economy rises from $2,678 per full-time worker[3] in 1929 to $7,236 in 1965 (in constant 1958 dollars). The sources of the near tripling of the marginal product of labor are divided between improvements in disembodied technical progress—42.3 percent; technical progress embodied in labor, or human capital—29.9 percent; and the increased quantity and quality of the capital stock—30.1 percent (see Table 3-1). The contribution of capital can be further divided into a 5.4 percentage point contribution from increases in quantity and a 24.7 percentage point contribution from increases in quality. Capital growth, labor growth, and disembodied technical progress account for slightly more than 100 percent of the net increase in the marginal product of labor, since two factors lead to a slight deterioration. A deterioration in the utilization rate between 1929 and 1965 led to a decline of 0.3 percentage point,[4] and a larger quantity of labor to a decline of 2.0 percentage points.[5]

The calculated marginal product of $7,236 for 2,000 hours of work in 1965 applies to the economy's average worker. If an individual possesses skills and knowledge above the average, his marginal product will be above average. If his skills and knowledge

[3] Full-time work means 2,000 hours of work per year.

[4] An explicit utilization factor must be included in the production function, even though only employed units of capital and labor are used in it. Since overhead capital and labor cannot be cut as drastically as production in a recession, the marginal productivity of labor automatically falls. The jobs which overhead workers are doing become less productive. Conversely, an improvement in utilization rates raises the marginal productivity of labor, since overhead workers become more productive. The marginal product of an additional worker is less when utilization levels are low.

[5] For a comparison of the sources of growth from the production function with the sources found by Denison, see App. A; they are generally similar. An effort was made to choose the best possible aggregate production function in order to study labor's marginal product, but economic knowledge is not yet adequate to dismiss alternative forms of the production function. The quantitative results are not definitive, but they do shed interesting light on the sources of growth of labor's marginal product.

TABLE 3-1

Sources of Net Growth in Marginal Product of Labor,
United States, 1929–65

(*In percentages*)

Source of growth		Contribution to growth
Technical progress embodied in labor		29.9
Disembodied technical progress		42.3
Capital stock (measured in efficiency units):		
Capital stock (measured in observed units)	5.4	
Technical progress embodied in capital	24.7	
		30.1
Utilization rates		−0.3
Labor stock		−2.0
Total		100.0

Source: Derived from marginal productivity equation discussed in text.

are below average, his marginal product will also be below. Technical progress and the accumulation of capital contribute to a rising marginal product for labor in the aggregate, but they do not have the same effect on every individual. Some workers may benefit; others may be hurt as skills and knowledge become obsolete.

Since differing mixtures of complementary factors are available to workers, there is a wide range of marginal productivity for labor. Theoretically the production function approach could be applied to each individual; his marginal productivity could be determined by knowing his human capital, his physical capital, and the efficiency of the sectors of the economy in which he works. The result would be a distribution of marginal productivities rather than a single average marginal product.

In an economy with perfect competition and in equilibrium, the distribution of marginal products is identical with the distribution of earned income. If employed workers are in poverty, they lack one or more of the factors leading to higher output. To eliminate poverty the deficiencies must be overcome. Each worker's low marginal productivity can be analyzed; when the causes are found, corrective or compensatory programs can be introduced to raise it. For those who are unemployed or underemployed, government programs might be needed to increase aggregate demand, raise labor's marginal product, and reduce unemployment—programs very different from those designed to raise the marginal productivity of those already working.

Analysis of the income distribution cannot stop with analysis of labor's marginal productivities. The theoretical equality of earned income and marginal products is based on the hypothesis that all markets are in equilibrium. In a dynamic growing economy, markets are never in equilibrium but are always adjusting to it. Incomes reflect the adjustment process as well as the equilibrium values of the marginal products. If innovations lead to sizable increases in the demand for the skills of a particular occupation, the wages in that occupation may rise above equilibrium levels to attract more people into the occupation during a transition period. Wages in declining occupations may fall below equilibrium levels until enough people have been forced out. This disequilibrium may be an additional cause of poverty which does not show up in the analysis of the marginal productivity of labor.

Imperfections and monopolies in the product and factor markets are another source of differences between the distribution of earned income and the distribution of marginal productivities. Labor's monopoly powers may lead to wages above marginal products in some occupations and wages below them in others. Imperfect knowledge may lead to inadequate market adjustments. Habits, customs, and attachments to geographic areas cause lags in adjusting incomes to current demands. Product monopolies may lead to underproduction of particular goods and the consequent distortion in the demand for labor to make these goods. If whites have monopoly powers vis-à-vis Negroes, or if Negroes are unjustly regarded as inferior workers, the market imperfection of discrimination may lead to Negro incomes below Negro marginal productivities.

A Poverty Model

Instead of using the indirect production function approach to estimate labor's marginal product, the relationships between poverty and the factors which produce poverty can be directly analyzed in

an econometric model.[6] In this section a model is developed to examine the incidence of poverty in each of the fifty states and the
District of Columbia. To isolate the interrelations between discrimination and poverty, the model is used to analyze poverty
among both Negroes and whites.[7] The same general model can be
used to explain Negro and white poverty, but discrimination plays
a major role in the incidence of Negro poverty.

In 1960, 21.4 percent of the nation's families were living on less
than $3,000, but this average masks a dispersion in the incidence
of poverty ranging from a high of 51.6 percent in Mississippi to a
low of 9.8 percent in Connecticut.[8]

The incidence of poverty in each of the fifty-one areas is explained by the percentages of (1) families living on farms,[9] (2)
families headed by a Negro, (3) families with no one in the labor
force, (4) family heads with less than eight years of education, (5)
population working full time, and by (6) the industrial structure
of the state and (7) a dummy variable necessary to correct for
Alaska and Hawaii, which have large numbers of nonwhites who
are not Negroes.[10] The equation reads as follows (a critique of

[6] The poverty model reverts to the $3,000 definition of family poverty. State-by-
state data do not exist on the official definition of poverty discussed in Chap. 2.
Only families are considered in the poverty model, but the same techniques could
be used for unrelated individuals.

[7] All data on Negroes actually refer to nonwhites. Since nonwhites are 92 percent
Negro, the text will use Negro and nonwhite interchangeably. U.S. Bureau of the
Census, *U.S. Census of Population: 1960*, Vol. 1, *Characteristics of the Population*,
Pt. 1, *United States Summary* (1964), p. xlii.

[8] *Ibid.*, p. 249. See also Lester C. Thurow, "The Causes of Poverty," *Quarterly
Journal of Economics*, Vol. 81 (February 1967), pp. 39–57.

[9] The proper poverty line for farmers is a subject of intense controversy. In the
1964 official definition of poverty the line for a four-person farm family was $1,925
and, as noted earlier, $3,130 for an urban family. The difference reduces the inci-
dence of farm poverty by approximately 40 percent. Mollie Orshansky, "Counting
the Poor: Another Look at the Poverty Profile," *Social Security Bulletin*, Vol. 28
(January 1965), pp. 9, 28.

The official difference is based on the food budget analysis mentioned in Chap. 2,
with all expenditures assumed to be proportional to food expenditures. If income-
in-kind reduces average farm expenditures for food by 38.5 percent, all other expenditures are assumed to fall by the same amount. The dubious nature of this
assumption, the disutilities associated with earning income in kind, and the fact that
many farmers do not raise their own food because of climate or specialization leads
me to opt for the $3,130 poverty line for farmers in preference to a lower line.

[10] The basic data for the poverty model are from U.S. Bureau of the Census, *U.S.*

the poverty model will be found in Appendix B):

(3-1) $P = a + bF + cN + dL + eE - fW - gI - hD + u$

where

  P = percentage of families in poverty (income less than $3,000)
  F = percentage of families living on farms
  N = percentage of families headed by a nonwhite
  L = percentage of families with no one in the labor force
  E = percentage of family heads with less than eight years of school completed
  W = percentage of population fourteen years old and above who worked 50–52 weeks per year
  I = an index of the industrial structure of the state[11]
  D = dummy variable for Alaska and Hawaii
  u = error term.

The variables in the poverty model are patterned after the factors that have significant effects on the marginal productivities of labor and on differences between incomes and marginal products. Identical variables cannot be used because of lack of data, but proxy variables can be found to represent the same effects. Thus education is a measure of the quality of human capital; full-time work is a measure of the effectiveness of government policies in translating potential productivity into actual productivity; the percentage of families with no one in the labor force is a measure of the families who are outside of the productive economy; the percentage of farmers and the industrial index are a measure of capital-labor ratios and organizational efficiency; the percentage of Negro families represents part of the impact of discrimination.

Census of Population: 1960, and *Current Population Reports,* Series P-50 and P-60. Specific sources are given in the footnotes and tables that follow.

  [11] The index is defined as follows:

$$I = \sum_{i=1}^{n} W_i X_i$$

where

  W_i = percentage of the state's labor force in industry i
  X_i = the ratio of the U.S. median income in industry i to the general U.S. median income. This index measures the prevalence of high wage industries in the state.

Given the current theoretical and empirical knowledge of poverty, equation (3-1) cannot be considered a structural model, since causation presumably does not move solely from independent to dependent variables. Low education levels and a poor industrial structure may lead to a high incidence of poverty, but poverty in turn leads to low education levels and to a poor industrial structure. Breaking the circle is difficult, conceptually, statistically, and from a policy standpoint.

Traditionally, median incomes are important explanatory variables in analyses of poverty (see Appendix C). Statistically they are, but they do not provide any information about the sources of income growth. The variables included in the poverty model have the advantage of providing some insights into those sources. Although the variables are more basic than median incomes, the model does not explain why the explanatory variables themselves vary from region to region. Further investigation of locational factors would be necessary to determine why industries with high efficiency levels and high capital-labor ratios locate in one area and those with low efficiency and capital levels locate in other areas. The health and age structure of the population may explain why families are outside the labor force. Some of these factors will be investigated in succeeding chapters, but the poverty model is designed to isolate the major causes of poverty and to provide a rough idea of their quantitative importance. The regression coefficients for each of the variables provide estimates of the potential gains that could be made by altering the size of the variable or the regression coefficient itself. Thus farm programs can be used to reduce poverty by reducing the number of farmers, but they can also reduce it by raising farm income levels and reducing the size of the regression coefficient of farmers. A rough idea of gross benefits can be obtained from the model, but a much more detailed investigation of the costs of particular programs to alter the explanatory variables or their coefficients would be necessary to provide estimates of net benefits.

None of the explanatory variables are direct government instruments of control. If the effects of the variables are to be altered, government policies must select instruments to change the size of the variable or its coefficient. For example, fiscal policies might be used to change the proportion of full-time workers, and antidiscrimination laws might be used to affect the size of the regression coefficient for nonwhites.

Using equation (3-1) in a weighted regression gives the following results:[12]

(3-1a) $P = 96.5125^{**} + 0.2978F^{**} + 0.1133N^{*} + 0.5410L^{**}$

$\qquad$ (23.1516) $\quad$ (0.0978) $\qquad$ (0.0544) $\qquad$ (0.1677)

$\qquad$ $+ 0.4345E^{**} - 0.5368W^{**} - 0.7600I^{**} - 10.3777D^{**}$

$\qquad$ (0.0480) $\qquad$ (0.1117) $\qquad$ (0.1978) $\qquad$ (4.8210)

$\qquad$ $\overline{R}^2 = 0.98$ $\qquad$ d.f. $= 43$ $\qquad$ $S_e = 2.3$

Note: The standard errors of the coefficients are shown in parentheses.
* Coefficient significant at 0.05 level.
** Coefficient significant at 0.01 level.

The poverty regression indicates that most of the variance in the incidence of poverty from state to state can be explained in terms of these seven variables (see Table 3-2). Based on an investigation of errors, there were no significant regional biases. All but one of the explanatory variables is significant at the 1 percent level, and that one is significant at the 5 percent level. All of the coefficients have the signs that would be expected theoretically. For each percentage point alteration that government programs can make in the independent variables, the model suggests that poverty would be reduced by the following percentage points: facilitating farm migration, 0.3; attracting families into the labor force, 0.5; lowering the number of family heads with less than an eighth grade education, 0.4; shifting workers from part-time to full-time jobs, 0.5; and improving the industrial structure, 0.8. For nonwhites the goal is not to change the size of the independent variable but to

[12] Since the dependent variable and most of the independent variables are in percentage terms, weights need to be attached to the different observations in regression (3-1a). A given percentage error will be much more serious in a large state than in a small state. Thus the observations in regression (3-1a) are weighted by the population of the state. Weighting by population rather than the number of families has the advantage of giving more weight to the states with larger families, but the two sets of weights are very similar.

The large intercept term is a scaling factor in the weighted regression. It does not indicate anything about the incidence of poverty.

Data used in the regression are from the same sources as those for Table 3-2.

TABLE 3-2

Range of Data for Variables Used in Poverty Model, 1960

(*In percentages*)

Variable	United States	Range among states	
		High	Low
Families living on farms	7.4	31.3	0.0
Families headed by a nonwhite	9.4	64.2	0.1
Families with no one in the labor force	10.7	24.7	7.5
Family heads with 0–7 years of school completed	21.9	45.0	8.0
Population aged fourteen and over who worked 50–52 weeks per year	34.8	47.4	27.2
Index of industrial structure	98.9	103.1	83.9
Incidence of poverty (families)	21.4	51.6	9.8

Sources: U.S. Bureau of the Census, *U.S. Census of Population: 1960*, Vol. 1, *Characteristics of the Population*, Pt. 1, *United States Summary* (1964), pp. 249, 269, 281, 286, 463–64, 470, 761–62, and *General Social and Economic Characteristics*, Final Report PC(1)-1C through PC(1)-51C (1962), Table 50. The index of industrial structure is defined in note 11 above.

reduce the regression coefficient to zero. If eliminating discrimination and increasing investment in nonwhites could bring this coefficient to zero, poverty would fall by 1.0 percentage point. (For an investigation of the interrelations between explanatory variables, see Appendix D.)

The Seven Variables

In this section each of the explanatory variables used in the poverty model will be examined in detail.

FARMERS AND THE INDUSTRIAL STRUCTURE

Since there are no direct measures of state-by-state capital stocks and efficiency levels, the percentage of farmers and the index of industrial structure serve as measures of capital per worker and the level of disembodied technical progress. The validity of these proxies depends on the assumption that the two items are relatively homogeneous within industries. Insofar as industries are not homogeneous, the industrial structure (including farming) cannot serve as a good measure. Since empirical observations indicate that there are differences within industries (especially between North and South), inserting measures of the industrial structure into the model must be based on whether they are efficient explanatory variables and whether the coefficients are reasonable.

The positive regression coefficient for farmers indicates that urban-rural mobility is an effective means of reducing poverty. Outmigration reduces farm poverty and does not increase urban poverty by an equivalent amount. Assuming that a cross section of farm families leaves the farm each year, approximately 60 percent of poverty-stricken farm families leave poverty when they move. The result is a net increase in urban poverty but a net decrease in national poverty. For every percentage point reduction in the number of farmers, the incidence of poverty falls by 0.3 percentage point.[13]

The regression coefficient for the index of the industrial structure is large,[14] but even this underestimates the long-run impact of improvements in capital-labor and efficiency levels. Over time output per worker rises primarily from gains in productivity within industries rather than from shifts in the structure. As a result the coefficient of the index of the industrial structure rises as well as the index itself.

Although the regression coefficient is large and rising, the industrial structure does not change rapidly for the whole country. A similar index rose from 94 to 99 between 1947 and 1964. A faster rate of aggregate growth would have led to a larger change, but the industrial structure of an entire country is difficult to alter.[15] Thus efforts must be concentrated on improving the distri-

[13] In 1960 the incidence of poverty among farmers was 50 percent. U.S. Bureau of the Census, *U.S. Census of Population: 1960, General Social and Economic Characteristics, United States Summary*, Final Report PC(1)-1C (1962), p. 226. If the group of families leaving the farm had the average distribution of income, approximately 60 percent of those in poverty left poverty when they left the farm. If the movers were above average in income, more than 60 percent of those in poverty left poverty when they left the farm. If all those who left were in poverty, 30 percent of them were able to escape poverty by moving.

[14] An occupational index was constructed in the same manner as the industrial index, but the two were so closely related that the variables could not be used together. When the two were used together, the occupational index was not significant.

[15] The average rate of increase for the industrial index was 0.1 percentage point in recession years, 0.4 percentage point in nonrecession years, and 0.6 percentage point during the Korean war.

bution of capital-labor ratios and organizational efficiency levels as well as raising the averages for the entire country. This might be done by promoting labor mobility, regional development, or aid to low productivity industries.

FAMILY UNITS WITH NO ONE IN THE LABOR FORCE

Not surprisingly the coefficient for families outside the labor force is very large. Fifty-four percent of the families leaving the labor force end up in poverty although two-thirds of them have previously been above the poverty line. A shift in family status from working to nonworking almost triples its probability of being in poverty. As rising productivity draws workers who can benefit from economic progress out of the poverty pool, and as individuals live longer, those outside the labor force are becoming an increasingly important sector of poverty. In 1947 they constituted 16 percent of the total number of families with incomes below $3,000 (in 1963 dollars); by 1967 the figure was about 40 percent. Even in absolute terms the number of such families expanded by almost 1 million. Most of the expansion can be explained by the age-sex distribution of the population. In 1947, families with female heads had a median income of approximately 70 percent that of families with male heads.[16] By 1967, although the income of both groups had increased, the relationship had declined to 51 percent. In 1947 the median income for families headed by a person aged sixty-five or over was about 58 percent that of families headed by a person under sixty-five; in 1967, it was about 46 percent.[17]

EDUCATION

If the coefficient of education in the poverty model is correct, improvements in education are one of the most effective ways of eliminating poverty. According to the most optimistic projections

[16] U.S. Bureau of the Census, *Trends in the Income of Families and Persons in the United States: 1947–1964*, Technical Paper 17 (1967), pp. 56, 74, and *Current Population Reports*, Series P-60, No. 59, "Income in 1967 of Families in the United States" (1969), p. 41.
[17] U.S. Bureau of the Census, "Income in 1967 of Families in the United States," pp. 32–34.

of the Census Bureau,[18] the percentage of family heads with less than an eighth grade education will fall from 21.9 percent in 1960 to 15.9 percent in 1970 and to 11.1 percent in 1980. Among those in the working age group the decline is even larger. Part of the decline is caused by improvements in the education system and part by the death of elderly family heads with poorer education. On the basis of the estimated decline in family heads with less than an eighth grade education and the coefficient for education from regression (3-1a), improvements in education alone will reduce the incidence of poverty to 18.8 percent in 1970 and to 16.8 percent in 1980 if the economy is able to generate enough capital to equip a more highly educated labor force.[19]

Although low educational attainment proved to be a much better explanatory variable than median years of education,[20] it should be regarded partially as a proxy for improvements in all levels of education. The largest reductions in the incidence of poverty occur as individuals move up from the bottom of the education scale, but there are reductions at all levels (see Table 3-3). Thus, the size of the education coefficient in the poverty model partially reflects improvements in education above the eighth grade level.

To test the hypothesis that the impact of education may differ for groups which suffer from discrimination, the poverty regression was run with an interaction term between nonwhites and education $[(N)(E)]$ in addition to the variables already in the model.[21] This allows a separation of the impact on whites and non-

[18] U.S. Bureau of the Census, *Current Population Reports,* Series P-20, No. 91, "Projections of Educational Attainment in the United States: 1960 to 1980" (1959). Education of family heads is approximated from estimated changes in male education levels.

[19] If the benefits of education partially depend on relative levels of education as well as absolute levels of education, the gains will be smaller than those estimated here. Thus a tenth grade education may become as much of a handicap in 1980 as an eighth grade education was in 1960 because of rising average levels of education.

[20] The median number of school years completed was substituted for the percentage of family heads with less than an eighth grade education, but proved to be a much less effective variable. Other more complex variables (such as the percentage of family heads with less than an eighth grade education minus those with a college education) were just as effective but were not included since they did not improve on the results of the simpler index in the poverty regression.

[21] This possibility was suggested by Samuel Bowles of Harvard University.

TABLE 3-3

Incidence of Poverty by Education of Head of Family, 1967

(*In percentages*)

Educational level	Incidence of poverty
Elementary	
Less than eight years	31.0
Eight years	18.0
High school	
One to three years	11.5
Four years	5.9
College	
One to three years	5.2
Four years	3.8
Five years or more	2.9

Source: U.S. Bureau of the Census, *Current Population Reports*, Series P-60, No. 59, "Income in 1967 of Families in the United States" (1969), Table 14, p. 42. The incidence of poverty is based on families of four with heads aged twenty-five and over and annual money income below $3,000.

whites. When the percentage of family heads with less than eight years of education was used as the education variable, the interaction terms never proved to be significant. At this level of aggregation and for low levels, improving education seems to have equal potential payoffs for both whites and nonwhites.

The high rate of return and the similarity of returns for whites and Negroes at low education levels is confirmed by looking at individual census data. According to Hanoch,[22] there are major divergences between the rates of return for whites and Negroes at higher levels, but the rates of return for less than eight years are high for both. Discrimination affects the marginal returns to education for Negroes as education rises, but it does not seem to affect very low levels of education. Here the competitive handicap for both groups completely dominates the impact of discrimination.

FULL-TIME WORK

Full-time work is the variable inserted to measure the effectiveness of government policies to produce full employment. Unemployment is a more common measure but it proved less effective in

[22] Giora Hanoch, "An Economic Analysis of Earnings and Schooling," *Journal of Human Resources*, Vol. 2 (Summer 1967), pp. 310–29.

measuring the impact of aggregate demand policies.[23] Many of those living in poverty are not unemployed, but are underemployed or not in the labor force. In 1967, 19.7 percent of heads of families living in poverty were working full time; 50.7 percent were not in the labor force;[24] 26.7 percent were working part time; and only 2.9 percent were unemployed.[25] Since the percentage of full-time workers takes into account the number of part-time workers[26] and the labor force participation rates, as well as the number of unemployed workers, it is a broader measure of the employment characteristics of a labor market than is the unemployment rate.

Like the education variable, full-time work is partially a measure of the entire distribution of hours of work. As full-time work increases, the hours of work per week of part-time workers and the number of secondary workers rise. The result is less poverty among families where part-time work plays an important role in family income.

Like the regression coefficient for the index of the industrial structure, that for full-time work is large and rising. As average wage and productivity levels rise, the average income paid to full-time workers also rises. As a result, full-time work becomes increasingly effective as a means of escaping poverty. From 1956 to 1965 the incidence of poverty among families with a head employed full

[23] While the proportion of full-time workers is a better explanatory variable of the incidence of poverty than state unemployment rates, the same economic factors influence both. The simple correlation between the two variables is 0.81. In the five states with the lowest unemployment rates in 1960, the average percentage of the population working full time was 8.5 percentage points higher than in the five states with the highest unemployment rates. The average percentage of unemployment for the two groups of states was 2.9 and 8.3. U.S. Bureau of the Census, *U.S. Census of Population: 1960, United States Summary*, p. 269, and U.S. Bureau of Employment Security, unpublished data on state unemployment rates.

[24] Note that this category is not the same as "no one in the labor force." Workers other than the family head may be in the labor force.

[25] U.S. Bureau of the Census, "Income in 1967 of Families in the United States," pp. 45, 46.

[26] The number of part-time workers is partly a demand and partly a supply phenomenon. Demand and supply are closely interrelated, however. When the demand for part-time workers rises, secondary workers such as housewives come into the labor force. When the supply of part-time workers rises and full-time workers are in short supply, demand shifts to part-time workers. The number of part-time workers is closely correlated with the number of full-time workers.

time dropped from 12.2 percent to 6.7 percent (using the definition of income below $3,000 in 1963 dollars).[27]

NONWHITES

The coefficient for the percentage of families headed by a non-white is small in relation to the total number of poor Negro families. If being nonwhite were the only factor that leads to nonwhite poverty, nonwhites should account for only 4.7 percent of the total number of poor families, according to equation (3-1a). In reality, nonwhites in 1960 accounted for 21.1 percent of the total.[28] Many of the other factors in the poverty model adversely affect Negroes: they have less education than whites, are more likely to be outside the labor force, do not have an equal share of full-time jobs, and are located in areas with poorer industrial structures (see Table 3-4). All of these factors lead to a much higher incidence of poverty among nonwhites than would be predicted by the non-white coefficient alone. Thus the coefficient for Negroes represents only part of the handicap of being a Negro, and the other variables in the model include many of the long-run effects of discrimination that would have to be eliminated before Negroes achieve true equality.

The hypothesis that the different variables in the poverty regression have a homogeneous effect across race as well as across states could be tested by calculating the same poverty regression with data for Negroes and then for whites. If the regression coefficients were the same, the hypothesis would be substantiated. Since this test cannot be performed because the data are not available, an alternative is to insert national data for Negroes and whites into the poverty regression to see how the actual and predicted incidences of poverty differ. If actual and predicted values are similar, some evidence is provided that the same factors cause Negro and white poverty.

[27] U.S. Bureau of the Census, *Current Population Reports*, Series P-60, No. 45, "Low-Income Families and Unrelated Individuals in the United States: 1963 (1965), p. 11, and No. 51, "Income in 1965 of Families and Persons in the United States" (1967), p. 26.

[28] U.S. Bureau of the Census, *U.S. Census of Population: 1960, United States Summary*, p. 225.

TABLE 3-4

Contribution of Each Variable in Poverty Model to Difference
between White and Nonwhite Poverty, 1960

(*In percentages*)

| Variable | Characteristic | | Sources of poverty gap[a] |
	White	Nonwhite	
Families living on farms	7.5	6.6	− 0.3
Families headed by nonwhite	0.0	100.0	11.3
Families with no one in the labor force	10.5	12.9	1.3
Family heads with less than eight years of school completed	19.2	48.5	12.7
Population aged fourteen and over who worked 50–52 weeks per year	35.5	28.9	3.6
Index of industrial structure[b]	98.8	97.8	0.8
Incidence of poverty			
Projected	18.6	48.0	29.4
Actual	18.6	47.8	

Source: Computed from data in U.S. Bureau of the Census, *U.S. Census of Population: 1960*, Vol. I, *Characteristics of the Population*, Pt. 1, *United States Summary* (1964). The incidence of poverty, actual, is from pp. 1–594.
a. Nonwhite minus white.
b. The index of industrial structure is calculated by weighting the index of each state by the number of white and nonwhite families living in that state.

Most of the explanatory variables have very different values for Negroes and whites (see Table 3-4), but the equation projects very well the incidence of both Negro and white poverty. The projected and actual rates are identical for whites and differ by only 0.2 percentage point for Negroes (48.0 percent versus 47.8 percent), despite the fact that the incidence of Negro poverty is more than twice as high as that for whites. Both qualitatively and quantitatively the same variables seem to explain Negro and white poverty. Most (82 percent) of the difference between the incidence of white and Negro poverty is explained by the handicaps of being a Negro and of having a low education level.

ALASKA AND HAWAII

A dummy variable is necessary for Alaska and Hawaii, since neither fits into the pattern of the rest of the United States. Both states have a very high proportion of "nonwhites," but they are not Negroes and do not suffer from the same kinds of discrimination. Differences in price levels, cultural backgrounds, and a host of other characteristics separate these two states from the other forty-eight. The coefficient of the dummy variable indicates that if Alaska and Hawaii suffered from the same problems as the rest of the United States, their average incidence of poverty would be 10.3 percentage points higher than it actually was in 1960.

Some important sources of growth which occur over time have not been considered in the model. As has been pointed out, there is no variable to measure productivity increases within an industry. As productivity levels rise over time, the coefficients of full-time work and the industrial structure will rise from their 1960 levels. The result will be an underprediction of the declines in poverty over time. From 1960 to 1965 the incidence of poverty actually declined by 3.6 percentage points in constant 1960 dollars,[29] while the estimated decline was 3.0 percent. The sources of the decline can be identified by using the poverty model. During those years increases in the proportion of nonwhite families and families outside the labor force would have led to increasing poverty, but they were more than offset by improvements in the other variables. Of the net estimated reduction in poverty, improvements in education accounted for 51 percent and the industrial structure (including farms) for 47 percent (see Table 3-5).

Summary

The causes of poverty are wider than the causes of low marginal productivities for employed workers. Other factors produce gaps between earnings and marginal products and leave some individuals completely outside the productive economy. To eliminate poverty will require programs to increase human capital, physical capital, and organizational efficiency, but it will also require programs

[29] Based on data from U.S. Bureau of the Census, *Current Population Reports,* Series P-60, No. 37, "Income of Families and Persons in the United States: 1960" (1962), and No. 51, "Income in 1965 of Families and Persons in the United States."

TABLE 3-5

Sources of Reduction in the Incidence of Poverty
between 1960 and 1965

(*In percentage points*)

Source of reduction	Amount of reduction
Farm families	−0.48
Nonwhite families	+0.05
Families with no one in labor force	+0.32
Family heads with less than eight years of education	−1.52
Population working 50–52 weeks per year	−0.43
Index of industrial structure	−0.91
Estimated decline	−2.97
Actual decline (constant 1960 dollars)	−3.6

Source: Estimated from the poverty model. For actual decline see note 29.

to correct market imperfections, lags in economic adjustments, and the status of individuals and families who are not now in the labor force. The marginal productivity of labor still plays a central role in the occurrence of poverty, however. The distribution of these productivities is a major factor in the distribution of income. Ideally, a study of poverty would have an explicit marginal productivity equation for each individual worker. Unfortunately, this approach cannot be used. No data exist on the physical capital available to particular individuals, the efficiency levels of the organizations in which they work, or the output which they produce.

Both production function analysis and the poverty model indicate that income levels and the incidence of poverty can be explained with the use of a very few general explanatory variables. Basically these are the same variables that have been selected on the basis of a priori knowledge and descriptive classifications of those living in poverty. The numerical values of the parameters from the poverty equation are also comforting. They indicate that investment in human resources, equal rights for Negroes, and the push to full employment can make significant reductions in the number of families living in poverty. Potential reductions do not become actual reductions, however, unless deliberate policy actions can affect the explanatory variables or their coefficients.

Variables such as education and discrimination have large potential effects, but the costs of changing these variables have not yet been determined. Preschool classes which result in fewer school dropouts will not increase education levels among family heads for fifteen years at best. Adult education programs must convince older individuals that they need to learn and can successfully do so. Attaining these goals will not be easy.

CHAPTER IV

Aggregate Economic Policies

Aggregate economic policies are important instruments in reducing both poverty and discrimination. Fiscal and monetary policies, by raising the level of aggregate demand for goods and services, can be used to stimulate higher utilization of economic resources; job opportunities for the disadvantaged expand, labor mobility increases, families are attracted into the labor force, and Negro incomes rise relative to white incomes.

The advantages of using aggregate economic policies to fight poverty and discrimination are many. Economic resources, instead of being used, are created. To expand production, private enterprise increases its investment in additional human and capital resources—for its own benefit. The happy by-product is less poverty and less discrimination.

This chapter explores the quantitative relationships between aggregate economic policies and the income distribution.

Utilization of Labor

Government policies to create tight labor markets are often advocated as instruments to reduce poverty. They are costless in terms of government expenditures and they produce rather than consume resources. According to their advocates, abundant job opportunities reduce poverty by providing employment and income for the unemployed, the underemployed, and those who are attracted into the labor market by the possibility of finding employment. In addition to quantitative employment effects, tight labor markets have beneficial qualitative effects. Shortages among skilled workers encourage businesses to enlarge training programs. Restrictive union practices may decline when workers are less fearful of competition for a limited number of jobs. As the probability of finding the desired job improves, individuals find it more profitable to develop skills and knowledge and become more willing to complete government training programs.[1]

Economists traditionally pay homage to the concept of a balanced labor market in which the vector of labor demands is equal to the vector of labor supplies. In such a market, however, there are no economic pressures leading to changes in either vector. If changes in the distribution of income are to occur, one of the vectors must first be altered. To create the pressures which can force the necessary structural changes, labor supplies and demands must be out of equilibrium: the demand must be larger than the supply. Shortages rather than balance become the *sine qua non* of progress, since they provide economic incentives for change.

The profit motive is the driving force behind business decisions. Business initiates change when it is profitable to do so. In an unbalanced labor market the employer's preferred workers are already employed and are no longer available. Since the employer cannot hire his preferred workers, he must investigate the profitability of hiring less preferred ones. Presumably he will hire the disadvantaged if the profitability outweighs the costs of hiring and training them. High utilization rates do more than reduce the supply of workers, however. Raising aggregate demand leads to shortages of goods and services as well as labor; the profitability of extra output rises, and with it the profitability of hiring disadvantaged workers.

[1] Labor shortages may also encourage the substitution of capital for labor. As long as government policies succeed in increasing aggregate demand to maintain tight labor markets, higher capital-labor ratios lead to higher average incomes, as employees work with more capital, but substituting capital for unskilled labor may also cause more poverty. Since the shortages will appear in skilled jobs, not unskilled, the pressure to substitute should be greatest at the skilled level, but some poverty may result from the dislocations of the substitution. In the long run, higher capital-labor ratios are necessary to raise the productivity levels of those in low productivity jobs.

An unbalanced labor market is similar to an economic boycott. Economic power is created in the latter by the employer's need for customer patronage, in the former by his need for labor. Both consumption boycotts and labor shortages create market power for the poor, but the durability of an unbalanced labor market is obviously greater than that of a boycott.

The magnitude of the structural changes caused by unbalanced labor markets depends on the length of time over which the market remains unbalanced. Long-run structural changes in obstacles to advancement and in methods of recruiting, training, and promoting should be even larger than short-run changes. Some supporting evidence for large long-run gains can be deduced from the income and employment changes which occurred during the Second World War, and from similar alterations in job content and in the erosion of artificial employment standards during the expansion of the late 1960s, but neither period is long enough for testing the long-run structural changes that would result from a prolonged period of unbalanced labor markets.

The prime evidence for long-run effects remains the existence of short-run effects. Both kinds of changes are caused by the same factors; the only difference is the time necessary to carry out changes and to recognize their desirability. If short-run effects exist, they probably become greater as the period under consideration lengthens. Factors which are fixed in the short run become alterable in the long run.

Queue Theory of the Labor Market

Increasing employment opportunities for the poor is one of the major ways tight labor markets alter the income distribution. According to the queue theory of the labor market, workers are arrayed along a continuum in order of their desirability to employers.[2] Employers choose their workers from as far up the queue as possible, but as the demand for labor expands, the divid-

[2] Desirability includes both objective and subjective elements. Objectively, workers should be ranked according to their potential marginal productivity, but subjective elements such as prejudice and ignorance can alter the objective ranking.

ing line between employed and unemployed shifts closer to the lower end. If a subgroup of the labor force is concentrated at the lower end for either objective or subjective reasons,[3] the subgroup's employment situation will be sensitive to the aggregate level of demand for labor. Employment expands when aggregate demand expands, and contracts when demand contracts; the popular phrase is "first fired; last hired." If a subgroup is concentrated at the top of the queue, changes in aggregate demand, unless they are very large, will have little effect on its situation, and it will remain employed.

The queue theory leads to three possible but not mutually exclusive hypotheses about the employment of disadvantaged workers and the expansion of aggregate demand: (1) When demand expands, the marginal employment gains among the disadvantaged will be relatively larger than those of preferred workers. (2) As the level of capacity utilization rises, the marginal gains in employment among the disadvantaged will become larger and larger relative to employment gains among preferred workers. (3) If capacity utilization is above some threshold, the disadvantaged will make large relative employment gains, but if it is below the threshold, there will be no gains.

Qualitatively the queue theory argues for operating the economy at very high levels of aggregate demand, but there may be associated costs, such as more rapid price inflation. To support policy recommendations, analysis must go beyond qualitative description and quantify the actual employment gains resulting at different levels of labor utilization. Without such quantitative knowledge, the benefits and costs of unbalanced labor markets cannot be evaluated.

The Queue Model

Since the queue hypothesis concerns relative rather than absolute employment gains, the gains of disadvantaged groups can be re-

[3] For a discussion of the possible causes, see Harry J. Gilman, "Economic Discrimination and Unemployment," *American Economic Review*, Vol. 55 (December 1965), pp. 1077–96.

lated to those of the corresponding preferred workers because the same factors influence employment for both. Thus employment gains for preferred workers can serve as a proxy for the expansion of aggregate demand when testing the queue hypothesis.

The unemployment rate among preferred workers is also one of the explanatory variables in the queue theory, providing a measure of how many preferred workers are left to be hired and of the demand pressures in the labor market. In the second hypothesis unemployment should be included in a nonlinear fashion, since the hypothesis implies that a decline in unemployment from 4 to 3 percent among preferred workers has a greater effect on the employment of the disadvantaged than a decline from 6 to 5 percent. In the third hypothesis preferred unemployment rates are relevant to the employment of the disadvantaged only if they are below some threshold.

In addition to the cyclical queue effects, there may be some autonomous trends working for or against employment of the disadvantaged over time. Less discrimination and more education may lead to larger employment gains for disadvantaged workers relative to those for preferred workers. Conversely, the skills demanded by business may be rising faster than the skills supplied by disadvantaged workers; as a result, their employment gains may become smaller and smaller.

Since finding a job is partially a random process, the greater the size of a disadvantaged group relative to the preferred group, the greater the likelihood of a member of the disadvantaged group finding the available job. Alternatively the structure of labor demands may adjust to changes in the vector of labor supplies, shifting to take advantage of the most abundant sources of supply. In either case, the employment gains of a group could depend on changes in its relative size.

In addition to labor's desirability, a group's position in the queue will be influenced by the wages which must be paid to it in comparison with the wages of the preferred group. In time series analysis of the labor market, the constancy of relative wages of preferred and disadvantaged workers precludes any testing of the impact of changes in relative wages, but it is possible to test for the impact of the minimum wage laws. Since the disadvantaged are concentrated in low-paying occupations where those laws have an effect, minimum wages may have a differential impact on the employment of preferred and disadvantaged workers.

Relative minimum wage variables rather than absolute minimum wages must be used to study the impact of such laws. As productivity and wages rise, a fixed minimum wage will affect fewer and fewer individuals; thus its employment effects will gradually disappear. Since the impact of a minimum wage depends on how much it compresses the wage structure at the bottom of the scale, the long-run effects of minimum wages must be studied by looking at the relation between them and average wages.[4]

Finally, lags may appear in the relationships between the employment of disadvantaged workers and the explanatory variables in the queue hypothesis. Based on a priori expectations, employment of disadvantaged workers would probably lag behind employment of the preferred.

The formal model is written as follows:[5]

$$(4\text{-}1) \quad E_t^D = a + \sum_{i=0}^{n} b_i E_{t-1}^A - \sum_{i=0}^{n} c_i U_{t-1}^A + \sum_{i=0}^{n} d_i (U_{t-1}^A)^2$$

$$+ e \frac{LF_t^D}{LF_t^A} + fT_t - g\left(\frac{MW_t}{AHE_t}\right) + u_t$$

where

E_t^D = employment of disadvantaged group

E_t^A = employment of advantaged group

U_t^A = unemployment rate of advantaged group

LF_t^D = labor force of disadvantaged group

LF_t^A = labor force of advantaged group

T_t = time trend

$\dfrac{MW_t}{AHE_t}$ = ratio of minimum wage to average hourly earnings

u_t = error term.

[4] Absolute minimum wage variables would be appropriate only if low wage jobs were completely isolated from increases in wages and productivity in the rest of the economy. If wages were not affected by the economy's wage level and workers could not move to higher paying jobs, the employment effects of minimum wage laws would not decay as average wages rose.

[5] Correlations in the model will be slightly misleading since LF_t^D includes E_t^D, but this is not a severe problem since LF_t^D is deflated by LF_t^A.

TABLE 4-1

Relationship of Employment of Whites, Nonwhites, and Teen-agers, Regression Results,
1954 through Second Quarter of 1966[a]

Group	Constant term	Employment of white group		Unemployment rate of white group			Ratio of nonwhite labor force to white labor force $\frac{LF_t^D}{LF_t^A}$	Ratio of minimum wage to average hourly earnings $\frac{MW_t}{AHE_t}$	Coefficient of determination $\bar{R}^2$	Standard error	Durbin-Watson statistic	Degrees of freedom
		E_t^A	E_{t-1}^A	U_t^A	U_{t-1}^A	$(U_t^A)^2$						
Nonwhite males aged twenty and over	-4370.6 (267.0) **	0.1419 (0.0163) **		-103.2 (35.1)		8.306 (3.898) *	300.95 (45.01) **	-2.588 (1.567)	0.98	28.0	1.08	42
Nonwhite females aged twenty and over	-2149.9 (162.4) **	0.1506 (0.0026) **		-17.55 (3.57) **			141.78 (12.31) **		0.99	18.5	1.23	44
Nonwhite teen-agers	-382.72 (96.77) **	0.0908 (0.0039) **			-4.5794 (1.2303) **		41.61 (2.99) **		0.92	12.9	1.93	44
All teen-agers	-1858.4 (272.4) **		-0.0272 (0.0076) **	-193.7 (51.3) **		14.603 (5.416) **	646.26 (23.05) **		0.99	39.9	1.56	43

Sources: Average hourly earnings were calculated from data in Survey of Current Business, various issues. Other data in the regressions are from U.S. Department of Labor, Bureau of Labor Statistics, Monthly Report on the Labor Force (November 1964), p. 15, and Employment and Earnings and Monthly Report on the Labor Force, various issues.
a. Employment is measured in thousands and the other variables in percentages. Figures in parentheses are the standard errors of the coefficients.
* Indicates statistical significance at 0.05 level.
** Indicates statistical significance at 0.01 level.

Negro Employment Gains

The queue theory can be applied to the employment problems of any disadvantaged group, but the quantitative effects will vary. Here the model is applied to black employment.[6] Since Negroes suffer from prejudice, low education and training, and a very high incidence of poverty, they qualify as a disadvantaged group in the labor force.

In order to create relatively homogeneous groups for testing the queue hypothesis, the labor force is divided into three groups—adult males aged twenty and over, adult females aged twenty and over, and teen-agers. These groups are distinguishable in terms of their unemployment rates and their employment distribution by both industry and occupation. Equation (4-1) is applied by regressing the employment of the disadvantaged on the variables of the corresponding preferred group. Adult nonwhite male employment is explained by adult white male variables, adult nonwhite female employment by adult white female variables, nonwhite teen-age employment by white teen-age variables, and total teen-age employment by adult variables (both male and female).

The results of applying equation (4-1) to seasonally adjusted quarterly data from 1954 through the second quarter of 1966 are shown in Table 4-1. The best equation is shown for each of the four disadvantaged groups. Variables were eliminated from the equation when their coefficients were not as large as their standard errors; however, all but two of the coefficients meeting this test are also significant at the 1 percent level. One is significant at the 5 percent level, and the other is considerably larger than its standard error.

Applying the queue theory to black employment problems, we come to the following conclusions:

1. There are few lags in the relationships. Employment of Negroes and whites moves closely together. Employment of nonwhite teen-agers is associated with white teen-age unemployment in the previous quarter, and teen-age employment is associated

[6] The model is also applied to teen-agers, since they must be considered in order to investigate the problems of Negro teen-agers.

with adult employment in the previous quarter, but no other lags are found. Various experiments were made with distributed lags, but they did not prove to be fruitful. Judging from the corrected $\bar{R}^2$s, the expansion of aggregate demand seems to affect the employment of both the advantaged and disadvantaged at the same time or with short time lags.

2. Although expanding employment among preferred white workers is associated with expanding employment for the corresponding less preferred Negro workers, the magnitude of the effects differs widely. The elasticities of Negro employment with respect to white employment (evaluated at the means) are 1.4 for adult nonwhite males, 1.0 for adult nonwhite females, 0.8 for nonwhite teen-agers, and 0.3 for teen-agers. If the expansion of aggregate demand represented by preferred employment gains were the only factor affecting disadvantaged employment, the employment gap between the white and nonwhite adult males would narrow; the gaps for nonwhite teen-agers and nonwhite adult females and the corresponding preferred groups would remain roughly constant; and the gap between teen-agers and adults would widen rapidly.

3. Employment of Negroes rises as white unemployment rates fall. For nonwhite adult females and for nonwhite teen-agers, a 1 percentage point decline in unemployment for the corresponding preferred white group results in employment gains of 0.7 percent and 0.9 percent, respectively. In the case of teen-agers and nonwhite adult males, the relationship is significantly nonlinear. A decline in white adult male unemployment from 6 to 5 percent raises nonwhite adult male employment by 0.3 percent, but a decline from 3 to 2 percent raises it by 1.6 percent. For teen-agers a decline in adult unemployment from 6 to 5 percent raises teen-age employment by 0.7 percent, but a decline from 3 to 2 percent raises it by 2.4 percent.

In the years under consideration the lowest unemployment rates for the preferred groups occurred at the end of the period. If the equations were used to predict nonwhite and teen-age employment gains for the third and fourth quarters of 1966, underpredictions might provide evidence to substantiate the threshold hypothesis. In no case, however, did employment rise substantially faster than expected. Perhaps the threshold hypothesis is correct and unemployment rates between 1954 and 1967 have simply not been low enough, or perhaps they have not been at those levels long enough. Both of these possibilities must remain open questions in the absence of sufficient data.

4. To find the total effect of expanding aggregate demand on Negro employment, the effects of both the employment and unemployment variables for whites must be added together. Some of the impact of expanding aggregate demand is measured by the direct association between Negro employment and white employment, and some by the association between Negro employment and white unemployment.

When both effects are combined, they substantiate the first hypothesis. Employment gains among Negro workers are larger than those among white workers for each age and sex group. If induced increases in the size of the white labor force are ignored, a 1 percent increase in adult white female employment and the corresponding reduction in unemployment results a rise of 1.7 percent in adult nonwhite female employment.[7] A 1 percent rise in white teen-age employment results in an increase of 1.5 percent in nonwhite teen-age employment.

Due to the nonlinear effects for adult nonwhite males and for teen-agers, their employment gains depend on initial unemployment levels for adult white males and for adults. If unemployment among adult white males is 2.2 percent and among adults is 2.9 percent, a 1 percent rise in adult white male employment would lead to an increase of 3.3 percent in adult nonwhite male employment, and a 1 percent rise in adult employment would result in a 2.7 percent increase in teen-age employment. For adult nonwhite males and for teen-agers both the first and second hypotheses are substantiated. As total unemployment falls, their employment gains become larger and larger relative to the employment gains of preferred workers.

5. No autonomous time trends were found for any of the four groups—either for the entire period or for various subperiods. The

[7] A 1 percent rise in employment results in a 1 percentage point reduction in unemployment in cases where unemployment rates are small, but not in cases where unemployment rates are high.

employment position of Negroes seems to be neither improving nor deteriorating.[8] On the aggregate level there is no evidence that any of the attempts to eliminate employment discrimination and to improve Negro or teen-age job opportunities have had significant effects. Examination of error terms in recent years does not reveal consistent underestimation of Negro employment gains.

6. As the relative size of a disadvantaged group grows, its employment gains also grow. Although changes in the relative size of advantaged and disadvantaged groups are potentially important for all four groups, large changes occurred only in the teen-age labor market. The teen-age labor force rose from a low of 7.6 percent (1955 I) to a high of 11.3 percent (1966 II) of the adult labor force, and the nonwhite teen-age labor force fell from a high of 15.6 percent (1955 IV) to a low of 11.9 percent (1965 IV) of the white teen-age labor force.[9] For each group there were important market changes proportional to the relative size of the advantaged and disadvantaged groups. If the increase in the relative size of the teen-age labor force had not been accompanied by market adjustments, teen-age unemployment would have been three times greater. Conversely, if the white teen-age labor force had not grown faster than the Negro counterpart, Negro teen-age unemployment would have been 5 percentage points lower.

7. Minimum wages were significant only for adult Negro males. Given the coverage that existed until 1967, minimum wages played no part in any deterioration of the employment picture for teen-agers as compared with adults, Negro teen-agers with white teen-agers, or Negro adult females with white adult females. It should be emphasized, however, that the model is testing for relative and not absolute effects. Adverse employment effects may exist, but they affect whites and Negroes equally.

Although the minimum wage variable is significant for adult Negro males, its effect is small. A 1 percent increase in the minimum wage relative to average hourly earnings causes a reduction of 0.07 percent in Negro employment. The income effects of mini-

<hr>

[8] Structural changes could appear in changes in the coefficients of the employment and unemployment variables as well as in a time trend, but the high $\bar{R}^2$s indicate that they were reasonably stable over the period under consideration.

[9] See Table 4-1 for source.

mum wage laws obviously outweigh the employment effects, although the individuals who receive the income gains are not those who suffer from induced unemployment.

Projections

Expanding aggregate demand to raise employment among the advantaged groups (adult white males and females) by 1 percent above 1966 levels would increase employment among adult non-white males by 3.3 percent, adult nonwhite females by 1.7 percent, nonwhite teen-agers by 3.9 percent, and white teen-agers by 2.6 percent. Gains of this magnitude would almost equalize adult male unemployment (1.2 percent for adult white males versus 1.7 percent for adult nonwhite males) and would improve the situation for other groups. There would still be a discouraging gap between black and white teen-agers and between teen-agers and adults, however (Table 4-2). If the level of unemployment necessary for the operation of the threshold hypothesis were to be reached, Negro employment gains might be larger and more equalizing, but there is no evidence indicating either the existence of this threshold or its location.

Perhaps the problem can be put into perspective by looking at white and nonwhite unemployment in 1953. National unemployment reached its postwar low of 2.9 percent. Unemployment for nonwhites was 4.7 percent, for whites 2.8 percent.[10] There is some evidence of a deterioration in the position of nonwhites since 1953, but this is entirely due to deterioration in the position of both white and Negro teen-agers.

The large relative employment gains predicted for Negro workers by advocates of unbalanced labor markets certainly exist, but the impacts are not constant across age-sex groups. Unbalanced markets have large favorable effects on the employment of adult nonwhite males, but less effect on the employment of teen-agers. The small extent of the teen-age employment gains means that some means other than aggregate demand techniques must be used

[10] These rates have been adjusted for the 1957 change in the definition of unemployment.

TABLE 4-2

Unemployment Rates for Adults and Teen-agers, by Color and Sex; Actual and Projected under Assumption of Expanded Aggregate Demand, 1966

Color and sex	Actual, second quarter 1966	Projected, 1966[a]
White		
Adult males	2.2	1.2
Adult females	3.4	2.4
Teen-agers	11.1	9.8
Total	3.5	2.4
Nonwhite		
Adult males	4.8	1.7
Adult females	6.3	4.7
Teen-agers	26.7	23.8
Total	7.5	5.0
Total white and nonwhite	3.9	2.7

Source: U.S. Bureau of Labor Statistics, *Employment and Earnings and Monthly Report on the Labor Force*, Vol. 13 (July 1966), pp. 103–04. Data are seasonally adjusted.

a. Projected under the assumption that aggregate demand expands sufficiently to raise adult white employment by 1 percent in 1966.

to solve the teen-age employment problem. Unbalanced labor markets can, however, be a major instrument for improving the employment position of adult Negroes.

Negro Income Gains

Because of the effects on personal independence and self-respect, employment opportunities are goals in themselves, but the ultimate policy objective is to alter the income distribution. Cyclical movements in the utilization of economic resources affect relative white and Negro incomes as well as relative employment gains. The long-run secular growth of family income is modified by two cyclical variables. Incomes vary directly with employment levels and inversely with the share of output going to personal income, as seen in equation (4-2). Since employment levels rise and the share going to personal income falls as aggregate demand expands, the cyclical factors work in opposite directions, but they have mutually reinforcing effects on white-Negro income differentials.

Although employment levels and income shares influence family incomes, the long-run growth of those incomes is determined by the growth of productivity. All of these factors are embodied in the following equation, which is used to explain the movements of both black and white family incomes:

$$(4\text{-}2) \qquad \ln M_t = a + b \ln P_t + c \ln E_t + d \ln S_t + u_t$$

where
M_t = median family income
P_t = GNP per employee
E_t = percentage of labor force employed
S_t = ratio of personal income to GNP.

The growth of productivity has the same long-run effects on both Negro and white incomes. The elasticity of median family income with respect to output per employee is slightly over 1.1 for both Negroes and whites. The cyclical parameters of the model differ markedly, however (see Table 4-3).

TABLE 4-3

Relationship of Median Family Income to Growth in Productivity,
White and Nonwhite Families, Regression Results, 1947–64

Median income	Constant term a	GNP per employee b	Percentage of labor force employed c	Ratio of personal income to GNP d	Coefficient of determination $\bar{R}^2$	Durbin-Watson statistic	Degrees of freedom	Standard error
White family	−0.882	1.140 (0.031)	1.209 (0.520)	2.353 (0.462)	0.998	0.78	0.14	0.02
Nonwhite family	−1.967	1.172 (0.070)	2.285 (1.157)	1.603 (1.023)	0.990	0.70	0.14	0.04

Sources: Derived from equation (4-2). Basic data are from U.S. Bureau of the Census, *Current Population Reports,* Series P-60, No. 51, "Income in 1965 of Families and Persons in the United States" (1967), p. 3; and *Survey of Current Business,* various issues. Figures in parentheses are the standard errors of the coefficients.

The income elasticity with respect to the personal income share is 2.4 for whites and statistically significant at the 1 percent level, but it is only 1.6 for nonwhites, statistically not different from zero. Since the share going to personal income rises in recessions and falls in expansions, the much larger positive elasticity for whites means that their incomes rise relative to those of Negroes during recessions and fall during expansions.

During a recession the incomes of both whites and Negroes can fall due to a decline in the utilization of the labor force, but a larger part of this decline is offset for whites than for Negroes. In fact, white incomes may continue to rise during recessions, as they did in those of 1958 and 1961. Unemployment insurance, the consistency of dividends, lower tax payments, and the other factors which contribute to the shift toward personal income in recessions are of much greater benefit to whites than to Negroes. The result is a cyclical deterioration in the relative income position of Negroes.

The cyclical income shift is exacerbated by different coefficients for the utilization of the labor force. The results show that a fall in the aggregate level of employment has almost twice as much effect on Negro as on white incomes (the elasticities are 2.24 versus 1.21). Negro incomes fall almost twice as fast as white, since Negro unemployment rises twice as fast. In expansions the relations are reversed and Negroes make large relative income gains. This is precisely what would be expected from the queue theory presented earlier.

Between 1947 and 1952 median nonwhite family incomes rose from 51 to 57 percent of median white family incomes, but by 1958 all of the gains were lost and nonwhite incomes were back to 51 percent.[11] With high unemployment and fewer opportunities, Negroes found jobs increasingly difficult to obtain. During every recession in the postwar period, the ratio of nonwhite to white incomes dropped sharply. With improving employment opportunities in the mid-1960s, nonwhite incomes rose to 55 percent of white incomes, and by 1967 they were slightly above 1952 levels. As the economy moves toward full employment, nonwhite incomes

[11] U.S. Bureau of the Census, *Current Population Reports*, Series P-60, No. 53, "Income in 1966 of Families and Persons in the United States" (1967), p. 4.

rise more than proportionately, but the equalization does not continue once unemployment stops falling. At a constant employment rate there is no tendency for general economic progress to narrow the gap in relative income. In absolute terms, the income gap widens.[12] Lowering national unemployment to 3 percent would reduce the gap between nonwhite and white family incomes, but eliminating the remainder of this gap would depend on other structural factors.

The difference between a tight labor market (3 percent unemployment) and a loose one (7 percent unemployment) results in a relative increase in nonwhite median family incomes from 50 to 60 percent of whites in the short run. In the long run the effects might be even greater. Although a 10 percentage point change in relative incomes does not eliminate discrimination, it represents an enormous improvement—especially when compared with the impact of any other policy instrument for altering the income distribution.

Reductions in Poverty

To illustrate the impact of an unbalanced labor market, this chapter has concentrated on the relative changes in the income and employment positions of whites and nonwhites as labor markets tighten. The same reaction patterns could have been observed by concentrating on the income and employment patterns for those

[12] If the economy were able to stay at full employment for several years, the parameters of equation (4-2) might change and lead to higher relative incomes for Negroes; but, as the equation stands, it conflicts with Locke Anderson's evidence that the gap between white and nonwhite family incomes would continue to close after full employment is reached. In his equation family income is simply made a function of per capita personal income. Since the coefficient for nonwhites is much larger than the coefficient for whites, Anderson concludes that general economic growth would reduce the difference between white and nonwhite median family incomes. His conclusions result from his failing to distinguish between trend and cycle. When allowance is made for cyclical changes, the coefficients of secular growth do not differ for whites and nonwhites. If Anderson's coefficients were correct, the postwar growth in per capita income should have led to much higher relative incomes for nonwhites. It clearly has not done so. W. H. Locke Anderson, "Trickling Down: The Relationship Between Economic Growth and the Extent of Poverty Among American Families," *Quarterly Journal of Economics*, Vol. 78 (November 1964), pp. 511–24.

with little education. During the economic expansion from 1964 to 1968 the unemployment rates for those with less than eight years of education declined much more than for those with more education.

Although large relative gains are made by Negroes in a tight labor market, their gains should not obscure the gains made by all of the poor. The national impact of tight labor markets on those below the poverty line, whether white or Negro, can be estimated from the poverty model in Chapter 3. The estimates are produced in a two-stage procedure. First, the impact of high rates of utilization on each of the explanatory variables is estimated. Second, the estimated changes in the variables are multiplied by their respective coefficients from the poverty model to obtain estimates of the reductions in the incidence of poverty.

In the model the percentage of the population holding full-time jobs was used as the direct measure of the utilization of the labor force. Although the proportion of full-time workers is a better measure of that utilization for the analysis of poverty, it is closely related to unemployment (the standard measure of utilization). Across states the simple correlation between these two variables is 0.81. In the five states with the lowest unemployment rates in 1960, the average percentage of the population who were full-time workers was 8.5 percentage points higher than in the five states with the highest unemployment rates.[13] Over time the same relationship is maintained. A reduction of 1 percentage point in unemployment results in a 0.75 percentage point increase in full-time work (Appendix E). Since the regression coefficient for full-time work is 0.54 in the poverty model, the direct impact of a 1 percentage point reduction in unemployment is a 0.4 percentage point reduction in the incidence of poverty [(1.0) (0.75) (0.54)].

In addition to its direct impact on poverty through improvements in full-time employment opportunities, an unbalanced labor market also has indirect effects on poverty through some of the other causal factors in the poverty model. The number of farmers, the number of families outside the labor force, and the

[13] The average unemployment rates for these two groups were 2.9 percent and 8.3 percent.

industrial structure are all affected by the level of aggregate demand.

Tight labor markets reduce the number of farmers by encouraging them to move into urban areas. When nonagricultural employment openings become available, farmers move to take advantage of higher urban income opportunities. An increase of 1 percent in the number of nonagricultural jobs leads to a 2.2 percent reduction in the percentage of farm families in the economy, and every 1 percentage point reduction in the proportion of farm families reduces poverty by 0.3 percentage point (Appendix E). On this basis, a 1 percent decrease in national unemployment would indirectly lead to a 0.1 percentage point reduction in the incidence of poverty by reducing the number of farmers.

Since individuals outside the labor force are attracted into the labor force by the availability of jobs,[14] tight labor markets also affect the variable for families with no one in the labor force. A decline of 1 percentage point in unemployment reduces the number of families with no one in the labor force by 0.4 percentage point (see Appendix E). Fewer families outside the labor force mean fewer families with poverty incomes. Every 1 percentage point reduction in unemployment indirectly reduces poverty by 0.2 percentage point through its effects on labor force participation rates.

Lower unemployment also affects the industrial structure; its index rises at a faster rate with a high level of utilization (Appendix E). The result is more high productivity jobs. A reduction of 1 percentage point in unemployment reduces poverty by 0.2 percentage point by increasing the growth of the industrial structure.

When the total impact of lower unemployment on full-time work, mobility, labor force participation rates, and the industrial structure is figured (Table 4-4), a decline in unemployment from 4 to 3 percent leads to a reduction in the incidence of poverty by 0.8 percentage point. Although such a decline does not eliminate poverty, it is large in comparison with the average year-to-year decline. From 1956 to 1966 poverty fell by 0.5 percentage point per

[14] Alfred Tella, "The Relation of Labor Force to Employment," *Industrial and Labor Relations Review*, Vol. 17 (April 1964), pp. 454–69.

TABLE 4-4

*Contribution of Various Sources to Reduction in Poverty Associated
with Decline in Unemployment from 4 to 3 Percent*

Source of reduction	Percentage contribution
Direct effects: increase in full-time work	54
Indirect effects	
Reduction in number of farmers	7
Reduction in families outside of labor force	20
Improvements in industrial structure	20

Source: Estimated from poverty model.

year.[15] Since the 0.8 percentage point decline is in addition to the
normal 0.5 percentage point, it represents a significant reduction
in poverty. One and a quarter million people emerge from poverty
when unemployment falls from 4 to 3 percent. In addition, many
of the benefits continue to accrue. The effects are not for one time
only: long-run effects continue to accelerate the rate of decline in
the following years. With productivity growing faster, incomes
grow faster.

Conclusions

Although the calculations of this chapter indicate that unbalanced
labor markets alone are not a sufficient answer to the problems of
poverty or discrimination, they present strong evidence that such
markets can lead very quickly to a substantial reduction in both.
Education, training, elimination of prejudice, and a host of other
policies are needed for a long-range final solution, but the unbalanced labor market is complementary to these and is perhaps a
necessary precondition for their success.

As a practical policy instrument, creating tighter labor markets

[15] In constant 1963 dollars. U.S. Bureau of the Census, *Current Population Reports*,
Series P-60, No. 45, "Low-Income Families and Unrelated Individuals in the United
States: 1963" (1965), and "Income in 1966 of Families and Persons in the United
States."

presents several advantages. Aggregate economic policies are impersonal. They can be implemented without recruiting a bureaucracy of administrators, trainers, teachers, and social workers. They do not require state and local cooperation. They do not interfere with personal choice. They can be quickly implemented; they are cheaply implemented; and they can become effective in a short period of time.

No one should be under the illusion that unbalanced labor markets are completely free goods. Some inflation would undoubtedly result (Appendix F). Steps such as price and wage controls might be necessary to offset the impact of inflation. Yet it must be clearly recognized that to be in favor of balanced labor markets, for the sake of price stability, is to be in favor of only small relative gains in the employment and income position of the poor.

CHAPTER V

Human Capital

Human capital (the skills and knowledge of the individual) is one of the key determinants of the distribution of income. Individuals with little education, training, and skills have low marginal productivities and earn low incomes. With very little human capital, they earn poverty incomes. Blacks who have less capital than whites earn less.

This being the case, more investment in human capital should help increase incomes. What might be called the productivity approach to the elimination of poverty and low Negro income is thus aimed at improving the quantity and distribution of human capital.[1] As a first step, the factors which create human capital need to be more clearly defined and quantified. To make the concept of human capital operational, it is necessary to specify the factors which cause increases in income and thus in human capital.

Income, Education, and Experience

With education serving as a proxy for human capital, the skeleton of the problem is revealed in Figure 5-1. The distribution of income is much more diffuse than that of education. There are

[1] Because of the many noneconomic benefits of education, the investment or human capital approach should not dominate either private or social planning for education and training. The human capital approach is justified, however, when education and training are being narrowly evaluated as instruments for improving the distribution of income. Here the only aim is to change income flows. Actual evaluations of education programs must consider benefits other than changes in the income distribution, but such benefits are beyond the sphere of interest of this book.

many more people with low incomes than with low educational attainment. If the distribution of education determined the distribution of income, there should be a greater number of individuals concentrated in the center of the income range. Other factors such as the distribution of intelligence, energy, or health may affect income distribution, but the figure shows that the same problem exists with respect to intelligence (IQ) : the distribution of income is again less concentrated. The large number of people in the lower tail of the income distribution cannot be explained by the distribution either of education or of intelligence, except in terms of a most peculiar cross-distribution.[2] The elderly and disabled can explain part; and interrelationships between intelligence and education can explain why there are some with very high incomes and others with very low ones. However, to isolate the factors which determine the distribution of income, it is necessary to go beyond the distribution of education or intelligence.

In practice, observed income flows are used to measure indirectly the value of an individual's human capital. People with higher incomes are assumed to have more capital. Consequently, the distribution of capital determines the distribution of earnings. Since this explanation is true by definition, it does not provide much insight into the causes of the distribution of earnings. The factors which create human capital still must be specified.

One procedure is to isolate all of the factors which cause differences in observed earnings and call them human capital. Another procedure is to narrow the definition, with only some of the factors termed human capital. The problem then is to determine the amount of the observed changes caused by these factors.

In this book, the narrow definition is used: human capital is acquired through formal education and on-the-job experience. The latter covers a wide range of activities; a major part of its value comes from formal and informal training programs. Another part

[2] Some people would have to be poor because of low intelligence and other people because of low education levels. If there were no overlap between the bottom parts of the intelligence and education distributions, there could be two independent causes of poverty to be added together. This still would not produce enough people in the bottom of the income distribution, but it is a step in the right direction. For this to be true, however, those with little education would have to be those with higher IQs; this is contrary to the usual assumption that those with the highest IQ have the most education. Education may also be a substitute for IQ, but this hypothesis would lead to a more nearly equal income distribution than that given by the distribution of either IQ or education.

FIGURE 5-1

Distribution of Income, Education, and Intelligence (IQ) of
Males Twenty-five Years of Age and Over in 1965

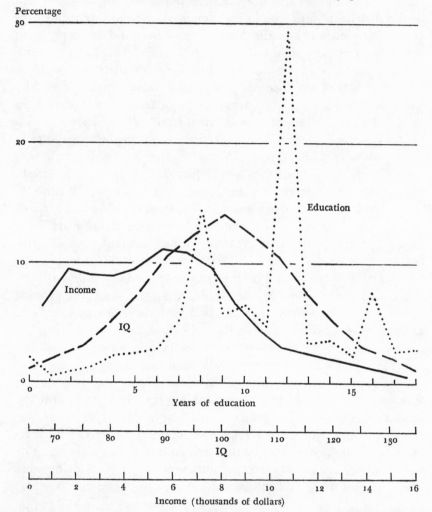

Sources: Income data from U.S. Bureau of the Census, *Current Population Reports*, Series P-60, No. 51 "Income in 1965 of Families and Persons in the United States" (1967), p. 34; education data estimated from U.S. Bureau of the Census, *Statistical Abstract of the United States: 1967*, p. 113; IQ data from David Wechsler, *Wechsler Adult Intelligence Scale Manual* (Psychological Corp., 1955), p. 20.

comes from general knowledge of how a particular business is run: where and when to report; what to do in case of emergency; familiarity with a particular group of jobs. All of these are factors that lead to higher productivities and are part of a man's total capital of skills and knowledge.

The value of human capital can be divided into price and quantity components. Education and on-the-job experience provide the principal means for increasing the quantity or quality of an individual's capital. Migration, improvements in information, and the elimination of market imperfections, such as prejudice, are the chief instruments to raise the price for existing capital. Although the price factor would not exist in perfect markets where all were paid equal amounts for the use of identical skills, in imperfect markets it is an important element in valuing human capital.

While price and quantity effects are theoretically distinguishable, in practice the distinction is blurred by using observed income flows as an indirect measure. Price and quantity effects are lumped together as changes in value. In most cases this is not a serious problem, since both the individual and society are interested in raising the value of human capital. Real investment is usually necessary to alter either price or quantity. The basic problem is finding that investment which will earn the greatest return. It may be one to increase the quantity or one to raise the price.

The use of income flows as a gauge requires that efforts to measure the specific effects of one factor must make explicit allowance for the impacts of all other factors. For example, since innate ability (whatever it is and however it is measured) and education levels are probably linked, each of them contributes to the incomes associated with higher levels of education. If some correction is not made for ability, observed income flows will overstate the actual returns to education.

Similarly, since on-the-job training and education are associated,[3] the returns to more education will be overstated if the effects of training are not considered; and since training programs

[3] According to Jacob Mincer, on-the-job training in 1958 accounted for 54 percent of the total training costs of those with a college education, 46 percent for those with a high school education, and 69 percent for those with an elementary education. "On-the-Job Training: Costs, Returns, and Some Implications" (paper presented before the Exploratory Conference on Capital Investment in Human Beings, New York City, Dec. 1–2, 1961, sponsored by the Universities-National Bureau Committee for Economic Research), *Journal of Political Economy,* Vol. 70 (October 1962: Supplement), p. 55.

have associated costs as well as benefits, the error is compounded in calculations of net returns to education. The benefits from training are included in the returns, but the costs have not been added to the education costs. In the case of ability, clearly there are no associated costs to be deducted.

Various efforts have been made to separate the returns to education from results attributable to ability.[4] Less effort has been made to solve the problems presented by on-the-job training, which is not surprising. Practically no direct information is available on either its amount or its costs. The informal aspects of much of the training mean that there is no practical method of obtaining direct information. A great deal of it is acquired in the course of work and does not result from deliberate programs. Costs are involved, but they are difficult to estimate.

The problem presented by on-the-job experience goes beyond that presented by ability in another way. Since by definition innate ability cannot be altered, society and individuals want to know the returns to increasing education, a variable which can be altered. On-the-job experience and training also can be altered. It is important to know what *combination* of education and training yields the greatest net return.

Complementarities between Education and Experience

The standard technique for isolating the returns to any one factor, such as education, has been to hold all other explanatory factors constant and to note the remaining differences in observed income flows. Either regression techniques or detailed data are used to hold those factors constant. Both assume that the effect of each of the explanatory factors is independent of all others and that their separate effects are additive. Thus, the amount of experience is assumed to have no influence on the returns to education, and the returns to increasing both education and experience are assumed to be equal to the sum of the separate returns to increasing each variable independently.

[4] See Giora Hanoch, "An Economic Analysis of Earnings and Schooling," *Journal of Human Resources*, Vol. 2 (Summer 1967), pp. 310–29.

In fact, however, many of the explanatory variables which affect income flows are not independent but complementary. Returns are not additive but multiplicative. This may be clearly seen in on-the-job experience and education. The returns from experience depend partially on the trainee's level of formal education. Low education levels make some types of training impossible and other types expensive, but as the levels rise, training costs fall and the variety of training which can be given expands. These complementarities also work in the opposite direction. Most jobs require some knowledge which is peculiar to the job and is not or cannot be acquired in school. Without this experience, education is of little value. Education and experience combined yield larger benefits than the sum of the two.

The same kinds of complementarities can be seen between human capital and the amount of physical capital used by a worker. Education and training are of little value without physical capital with which to work, but physical capital is also of little value without the necessary human skills to operate it efficiently. Most training is designed to teach labor to operate some piece of mechanical equipment. Thus the returns to either physical capital or training depend on the quality of the other.

There are two main sources of complementarities. Those that are technological occur when the skills and knowledge acquired in school are complementary to those acquired in training. Price complementarities occur when market imperfections are reduced in the process of acquiring education and training: a black might receive a larger income if higher levels of education and training allowed him to move into occupations where less discrimination existed.

The degree of complementarity differs. In some jobs there is little; in others, education and training are rigidly linked together. A priori reasoning leads to the conclusion that complementarities are important, and the data presented below confirm this conclusion.

Ignoring complementarities leads to biased estimates of the returns to increasing education. Holding training levels constant while observing the returns to education may provide a valid estimate of the returns within each training level, but it provides a distorted view of the general returns, part of which arises from shifting training levels as well as from moving up the income ladder within each level. To estimate the returns while holding the level of training constant is to seriously underestimate the actual returns to education.[5]

Individuals receive formal and informal training while they are at work. The effect of one year of work experience on the value of an individual's human capital varies according to the amount of training received or the impact of work experience on the price of existing capital. While one year of work yields everyone one year of experience, the returns from that experience—the income flows produced by it—may be very different. If observed income flows are higher, the value of human capital has increased, as a result of increases either in the quantity of human capital or its price. If there are no price effects, income flows depend on the amount of skills and knowledge received. Thus the returns to a year of work experience can be used as a surrogate variable to measure the returns to investment in on-the-job training. If labor training markets are in equilibrium, the rates of return on training will be equal for all formal and informal training projects; in this case different returns to experience would reflect different amounts of investment in on-the-job training, since equal investments would earn equal returns. If labor training markets are not in equilibrium this will not be true, but the returns to experience still indicate the pattern of gross benefits from training. The function simply measures the gross returns to a year of work experience.

The Human Capital Function

A precise functional relationship must be determined between the value of human capital and its explanatory factors. This is here termed the human capital function. All of the factors that increase incomes must be considered and their interactions specified. This analysis concentrates on the joint impact of formal education and

[5] This is equivalent to holding occupations constant while studying the returns to education. Many of the returns occur by moving across occupations rather than within occupations.

on-the-job experience—the major instruments for altering the quantity of human capital.[6]

The empirical work presented below is not definitive, since all of the relevant explanatory factors have not been considered, most notably innate ability. The work does, however, confirm the need for a human capital function and its precise specification. The complementarities between education and experience are large and should not be ignored in evaluating programs to alter income distribution by changing the distribution of either factor. For males in the American economy the returns to both education and experience are approximately four times as large as the sum of the returns to each of them separately. The observed price differences across race, occupation, and region are also large. For Negroes these price differences severely reduce the complementarities between education and experience as well as the absolute returns to either.

A function analogous to the production function can be constructed for human capital:

$$(5\text{-}1) \qquad\qquad I_{ik} = A\,Ed_i^b\,Ex_k^c$$

where

I_{ik} = income for an individual with i years of education and k years of experience

A = shift coefficient

$Ed_i = i$ years of education

$Ex_k = k$ years of experience

b and c = income elasticities.

Just as the real variables and parameters on the right side of a production function determine the annual flow of goods and services, so do the real variables and parameters on the right side of the human capital function determine the annual flow of income produced by the stock of human capital. According to the human cap-

[6] See Lester C. Thurow, "The Occupational Distribution of the Returns to Education and Experience for Whites and Negroes," in *Federal Programs for the Development of Human Resources*, A Compendium of Papers Submitted to the Subcommittee on Economic Progress of the U.S. Joint Economic Committee, 90 Cong. 2 sess. (1968), Vol. 1, pp. 267–84.

ital function, income flows depend on the years of education and experience, the income elasticities with respect to education and experience (b and c), and a shift coefficient (A). Making the assumptions which were outlined above, the amount of on-the-job training is represented by the years of experience and the income elasticity with respect to experience. The shift coefficient represents the impact of different capital-labor ratios, the level of technical progress, discrimination, unionization, market imperfections, and any other relevant factors except education and experience (see Chapter 6). The shift coefficient differs among different groups and over time, but for any one group and at any point in time it can be regarded as a constant.

The impacts of education and experience on incomes can be found by taking the partial derivatives of the human capital function:

(5-2a)
$$\frac{\partial I_{ik}}{\partial Ed} = A b E d_i^{b-1} E x_k^c$$

(5-2b)
$$\frac{\partial I_{ik}}{\partial Ex} = A E d_i^b c E x_k^{c-1} .$$

As these derivatives indicate, the marginal product of education depends on the shift coefficient, the years of experience, and the years of education already completed. In the same manner the marginal product of experience depends on the shift coefficient, the years of education, and the years of experience already completed. As both of these functions indicate, the returns to either education or experience depend on the level of the other.

Since the income elasticities (b and c) are not constrained, there may be increasing or decreasing returns to increases in education and experience. If the sum of the two elasticities is greater than one, there are increasing returns; if the sum is less than one, there are decreasing returns.

There is also no reason why the elasticities should be constant over all ranges of education and experience. College may produce higher returns than high school. To test for such differences, the function can be disaggregated into different ranges of education and experience:

$$(5\text{-}3) \qquad I_{ik} = A \prod_{g=1}^{n} Ed_i^{bg} \prod_{l=1}^{m} Ex_k^{cl}$$

where
   n = education classes
   m = experience classes.

If the human capital function is fitted to actual income data, it can be judged by the standard statistical tests. These cannot be applied to the usual calculations of the returns to education. Observed income differences are adjusted for what are believed to be other relevant factors and education is assumed to be responsible for the residual. No statistical tests are possible on this latter assumption.[7] The human capital function, however, has the advantage of providing both statistical tests of its own validity and estimates of the empirical size of the relationships.

The Data

The human capital function was fitted to 1960 median income data for males eighteen to sixty-four years of age.[8] Functions were estimated for Negroes and whites in the North and South. For each group there were seventy-two income cells made up of different male age-education classes. Years of schooling completed were taken directly from census data. Years of experience were calculated by subtracting the age at which an individual started work from his current age. Each individual was assumed to have begun working at age eighteen if he had finished school by that age. If not, work began at the school-leaving age. Thus a college graduate was assumed to have started work at twenty-two. A worker fifty years of age had twenty-eight years of experience if he was a col-

[7] The additivity assumption can be compared with the human capital function (equation 5-1) by testing the equation $I = a + bEd + cEx$. The form of the function given in equation (5-1) does a better job of fitting the observed data. The additive model leads to negative incomes for groups with little education and experience.

[8] All data are from U.S. Bureau of the Census, *U.S. Census of Population: 1960, Subject Reports, Educational Attainment*, Final Report PC(2)-5B (1963). North includes West in the census classifications.

lege graduate, thirty-two years if he was a high school graduate. Eighteen was selected as the starting age for those with twelve or fewer years of education, since child labor laws and workmen's compensation laws prevent earlier entry into many jobs. In addition, the proportion of full-time workers jumps sharply at age eighteen.

To test the hypothesis that different ranges of education and experience have different elasticities, the education variable was divided into three variables (0–8 years, 9–12 years, and more than 12), and experience was divided into four variables (0–5 years, 6–15 years, 16–35 years, and more than 35). In a cross-sectional analysis of male incomes the human capital function worked very well. In all classifications 90 percent of the variation in incomes was explained (see Appendix G).

The Results: White versus Negro

Income elasticities with respect to education and experience were not constant for all levels of education and experience.[9] For white males the income elasticities were 0.11 for elementary education, 0.72 for high school education, and 1.73 for college education (see Table 5-1). For Negro males the elasticities were 0.08, 0.76, and 1.33, respectively—similar for secondary education, but smaller for elementary and college education. If reports on the demands for Negro college graduates are correct, the income elasticity for college education may have increased rapidly in the middle 1960s, but as late as 1960 Negro elasticities were much lower than those for whites.

Income elasticities with respect to experience for white males were 0.20 for the first five years, 0.71 for the next ten, and −0.09 for sixteen to thirty-five years. For Negro males the comparable figures were 0.26, 0.65, and −0.14.[10]

The shift coefficients are also lower for Negroes ($783) than for whites ($1,140), meaning that a given amount of education and ex-

[9] Income elasticities measure the percentage increase in annual incomes as a result of a 1 percent increase in education or experience.

[10] Age can cause skills to depreciate, and skills can become obsolete. Greater depreciation for Negroes may be due to lower health standards or less permanent skills.

TABLE 5-1

Income Elasticities of Education and Experience for Males,
by Color and Region, 1960

Color and region	Years of education			Years of experience				Shift coefficient
	0–8	9–12	Over 12	0–5	6–15	16–35	Over 35	
All white	0.11	0.72	1.73	0.20	0.71	−0.09	0	$1,140
All nonwhite	0.08	0.76	1.33	0.26	0.65	−0.14	0	783
Northern white	0.10	0.52	1.70	0.20	0.70	−0.06	0	1,278
Northern nonwhite	0.06	0.51	1.22	0.27	0.63	−0.11	0	1,013
Southern white	0.11	0.90	1.91	0.20	0.75	−0.21	0	702
Southern nonwhite	0.08	0.57	1.74	0.24	0.61	−0.26	0	709

Source: Derived from human capital function described in text. Northern includes West in the census classifications.

perience earns less. Thus blacks could have the same amounts of education and experience as whites and the same income elasticities with respect to education and experience, but still earn lower incomes due to smaller shift coefficients.

The annual marginal product of education and experience can be shown graphically. A word of caution is necessary, however. Since the coefficients of the human capital function are subject to error, so are the annual marginal products derived from them. In addition, breaking education and experience into discrete groups of years makes the discontinuities sharper than they in fact are. The data should be interpreted as indicating the general pattern of the marginal product of education and experience without worrying about the precise dollar value in each year.

Figure 5-2 shows that, for the average white male with twenty years of experience, the value of education falls from $1,277 per year for the first year to $57 for the eighth year, then rises to $967 for the sixteenth year. The returns to the average Negro are much smaller: $754 per year for the first year to $31 for the eighth year, rising to $461 for the sixteenth year. As education levels rise, the Negro falls further and further behind (see Table 5-2). With no education, his annual income is $483 lower than that for a white male with no education. With eight years of education he is $1,367 behind a comparable white; with twelve years he is $1,750 behind; with sixteen years he is $3,556 behind. The income gap grows as

FIGURE 5-2

*Marginal Product of Education for White and Nonwhite Males
with Twenty Years of Experience in 1960*

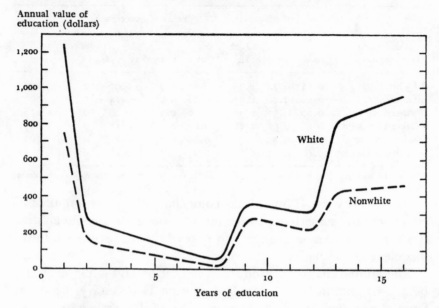

Source: See Table 5-1.

education rises, and at an increasing rate. The relative quality of
education may deteriorate as education levels rise, but discrimination probably hurts the better educated most.

This U-shaped pattern of the marginal product of education
would have been expected, given the existing distribution of education. Since the average male between eighteen and sixty-four
years of age has 10.5 years of education, men with little or none
are under extreme competitive handicaps when looking for work.[11]
Consequently, early years of education bring large increases in annual incomes, although they are smaller for Negroes than for
whites. After the large early returns, the marginal product falls

[11] Calculated from U.S. Bureau of the Census, *U.S. Census of Population: 1960*, Vol.
1, *Characteristics of the Population*, Pt. 1, *United States Summary* (1964), Table 173,
p. 404.

TABLE 5-2

Annual Income Gap Resulting from Increases in Experience and Education for Males, by Color and Regional Groups, 1960

(In dollars)

Twenty years of experience		Ten and one-half years of education	
Years of education	Income gap	Years of experience	Income gap
White in relation to nonwhite			
0	483	0	340
8	1,367	5	624
12	1,750	15	1,602
16	3,556	35	1,632
Northern white in relation to southern white			
0	661	0	113
8	1,130	5	422
12	682	15	677
16	593	35	1,194
Northern nonwhite in relation to southern nonwhite			
0	963	0	59
8	1,203	5	610
12	1,419	15	1,266
16	1,375	35	1,465
Northern white in relation to northern nonwhite			
0	102	0	339
8	1,177	5	440
12	1,462	15	1,324
16	3,267	35	1,427
Southern white in relation to southern nonwhite			
0	404	0	285
8	1,250	5	637
12	2,199	15	1,913
16	4,049	35	1,698
Southern white in relation to northern nonwhite			
0	−559	0	226
8	47	5	27
12	780	15	647
16	2,674	35	223

Source: See Table 5-1.

throughout the later elementary grades. With courses relevant to needed job skills, the marginal product rises slightly during high school years, but the large concentration of people with high school skills prevents the increases from being very large. With more relevant job skills and a smaller supply of people who possess college level skills, the marginal product during the college years rises sharply. For Negroes, however, there is only a slight increase in the marginal product of a year of education during the college years. This phenomenon may, of course, change if the pattern of discrimination changes, and it may have already changed, since this study is based on historical data.

Returns to experience do not show the same general U-shaped pattern (Figure 5-3). The value of experience is very high in early years, but falls off as the amount increases. For the average white male with 10.5 years of education, the marginal product of experience falls from $1,100 for the first year to $248 for the fifteenth year, to minus $12 for the thirty-fifth year. For the nonwhite male the corresponding amounts are $805, $157, and minus $13. The biggest gaps in returns to experience come during the early working years (see Table 5-2). A Negro with no experience and 10.5 years of education begins with an income $340 below that of a similar white. After five years he is $624 behind, after fifteen years $1,602, and after 35 years $1,632. Most of this gap is built up during the first fifteen years of a worker's career. During these years of high training investments, Negroes either receive much less training or are paid less than whites with the same skills. After fifteen years Negroes and whites are treated equally: neither group receives training.

The large marginal product of experience in the early years of work is easily explained. Workers learn how to perform in an industrial setting, they learn job patterns, they establish credentials and references, they discover how the labor market functions, and they put an initial period of trial and error behind them. Consequently, they are more valuable. Since this proficiency is quickly secured, the marginal product of experience falls sharply.

The increase between the sixth and fifteenth years is slightly harder to explain. This is the period when on-the-job skills are acquired. Workers have found jobs that will provide needed skills

FIGURE 5-3

*Marginal Product of Experience for White and Nonwhite Males
with Ten and One-half Years of Education in 1960*

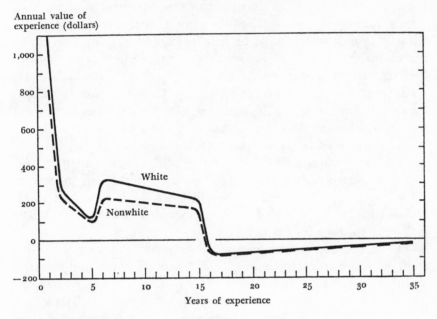

Source: See Table 5-1.

and have acquired the seniority to be eligible for them. Both formal
and informal training programs primarily benefit workers after
they have been in the labor market for a few years. Good jobs with
advancement possibilities are not open to those fresh in the labor
market.

After fifteen years of experience, the marginal product falls,
since workers do not learn new skills and added seniority does not
have a major impact on their job opportunities. Firms may not
wish to invest in older workers because of the limited time in
which their skills may be used. In addition, skills and knowledge
acquired at an earlier age may become irrelevant and obsolete.
Consequently, the marginal product of experience becomes small
and actually negative over some experience ranges.

North versus South

For a white male in the North with twenty years of experience, a high school education increases his annual income by $3,345 above what it would have been if he had had no education. The figure for a white male in the South is very similar—$3,324. For Negroes the comparable figures are $1,985 and $1,529. Although the marginal returns to education are similar in the North and the South, average incomes are much higher in the North. This fact is explained by higher shift coefficients and greater returns to experience. A white male with twenty years of experience and twelve years of education earns $682 more in the North than in the South. A Negro male earns $1,419 more. Obviously the incentives for a Negro to move north to benefit from the higher shift coefficients and more extensive or higher priced training are much greater than those for a white.[12]

The importance of experience can be seen by looking at the income gaps between North and South for both whites and Negroes as the level of experience increases (Table 5-2). For whites the gap rises from $113 for those with no experience to $1,194 for those with thirty-five years of experience. For Negroes the gap rises from $59 to $1,465 over the same interval.

In large part shift coefficients explain lower incomes in the South. The coefficient for whites is $576 lower in the South than in the North. For Negroes the figure is $304. High coefficients are primarily of benefit to northern whites. Interestingly, those for northern Negroes, southern whites, and southern Negroes are all very similar. Thus income differences between these three groups are explained primarily by education and experience.

Even more important is what happens when education and experience increase simultaneously. The whole is much greater than

[12] To gain the benefits of higher returns to experience, a Negro would have to move to the North to get the better training. Generally years of work do not become more valuable by simply moving north unless some training was received in the South. If discrimination were less in the North, the simple process of moving could make the training more valuable.

TABLE 5-3

Annual Increase in Income of Males Resulting from Education
and Experience, by Color and Region, 1960

(*In dollars*)

Color and region	Experience only[a]	Education only[b]	Experience and education[c]
All white	1,409	681	8,155
All nonwhite	1,148	244	4,856
Northern white	1,658	616	8,385
Northern nonwhite	1,702	144	5,260
Southern white	1,257	719	7,293
Southern nonwhite	811	252	3,724

Source: Derived from human capital function described below in text. Basic data are from U.S. Bureau of the Census, *U.S. Census of Population: 1960, Subject Reports, Educational Attainment*, Final Report PC(2)-5B (1963). Northern includes West in the census classifications.
a. Thirty-five years of experience, no education.
b. Sixteen years of education, no experience.
c. Thirty-five years of experience and sixteen years of education.

the sum of the parts.[13] If the effects were no greater than the sum of the two separate effects, thirty-five years of experience and sixteen years of education would raise white incomes by $2,090 above what they would have been with no education and no experience. In fact, sixteen years of education and thirty-five years of experience are worth $8,155—or almost four times as much as the sum of the separate parts. Similar complementarities exist for Negroes, though the absolute income levels are lower: three and one-half times the sum of the separate parts (see Table 5-3). Similar complementarities exist in both the North and the South.[14] (See Appendix H for a critique of the human capital function.)

Factors Underlying Acquisition

The importance of human capital—and especially of education and training—in raising incomes and eliminating poverty has been

[13] The same kinds of complementarities would exist between migration and education or training.

[14] For application of the human capital function to different occupations, see Thurow, "The Occupational Distribution of the Returns to Education and Experience for Whites and Negroes."

established. The next step is to consider the various elements to be taken into account when decisions are made regarding investments to increase human capital.

INDIVIDUAL DECISIONS

Individuals should invest in education and training as long as the discounted benefits exceed the discounted costs or as long as the internal rate of return from acquiring human capital is greater than the rate of return that can be earned from alternative investments:[15]

$$(5\text{-}4) \qquad \sum_{t=0}^{n} \frac{R_t}{(1 + r)^t} = \sum_{t=1}^{n} \frac{C_t}{(1 + r)^t}$$

where

R_t = stream of present consumption plus future earnings associated with an investment

C_t = stream of cuts associated with an investment

r = individual discount rate and risk premium.

According to the productivity theory of poverty, the stream of earnings produced by education and training is identical with the stream of marginal products they produce. But the identity is not important to the individual trying to increase his income; he is interested only in whether his investment will in fact increase his future earnings or present consumption, not in whether output will also increase.

The amount of investment by an individual depends on the size of his investment budget and his discount rate. If he faces a budget constraint, he may not be able to invest in his human capital to the point where the discounted returns are equal to the discounted costs. In theory, access to capital markets should remove budget constraints, but imperfect capital markets limit the ability

---

[15] Surface similarities between human capital investment and investment in physical capital should not be allowed to hide fundamental differences. Individuals are forced to accompany their investment in human capital, but not in physical capital. Thus noneconomic preferences become more important in human capital investment than in physical capital investment. Profit maximization makes more sense in physical capital investment than it does in human capital investment. Human capital also differs from physical capital in terms of liquidity. Physical capital may be sold, but human capital may not be. Thus the risks in human capital investment are higher.

of individuals to invest in their own human capital. Human capital cannot serve as collateral and borrowing requires collateral. Therefore borrowing does not remove the budget constraint. The impact of imperfect capital markets is particularly harsh on the poor. Their low current income levels lead to severe budget constraints. Since they do not even have the collateral of a good income flow, they cannot borrow from the capital markets. The poor may know that the discounted benefits of more human capital are much larger than the discounted costs of acquiring human capital, but still be unable to acquire more human capital. They simply do not have the resources to make the necessary investment.

Low incomes have another effect. They raise an individual's rate of time preference or his discount rate. As incomes fall, the marginal utility of current income rises. Since the poor have greater need for current income than the wealthy, they rationally cannot afford to devote as large a part of current income to producing future income and must therefore invest less in human capital.

The systematic difference in time preference between the poor and the wealthy is further compounded by differences in risk premiums. The poor are less firmly established in society, have less information about the labor market, and have less certainty that they will benefit from investment in human capital. For them personal investment takes on aspects of a risky speculation. They must add a high risk premium to their already high discount rate. The result is a further depression in the amount of human investment they are willing to undertake.

Insofar as individuals must rely on their own assets for human investment, the poor will fall further and further behind in the acquisition of human capital. They continually underinvest in their human capital since they lack the necessary assets. This lack is compounded by the high discount rates and high risk premiums produced by poverty. The result is that the least investment is made by the very groups that should invest the most if poverty is to be eliminated.

This analysis shows that rational private decisions can lead to a distribution of human capital which becomes less and less equal over time. To combat such an undesirable distribution, society may have to alter the pattern of private decisions. It has three instruments it may use. First, society can raise the incomes of the poor to lower their budget constraints and time discount rates. Second, it can improve individual knowledge of the benefits to be gained by increasing human capital; this lowers individual risk premiums. Third, it can provide subsidies to lower the private costs of training and education. These may be given directly to the individual or indirectly through public education and training institutions. To the extent that individual training costs are income foregone rather than direct expenditures, income supplements and training cost subsidies are almost identical.

DECISIONS BY PRIVATE FIRMS

Private firms are another major source of human investment. They invest in individuals since they find it profitable to increase the quality of their human labor force. The profit-maximizing firm provides training programs until the marginal returns and costs are equalized. If returns are greater than costs, more training is undertaken; if the reverse is true, less training is undertaken.

There are two sources of returns from training investments for private firms. (1) Profits can be earned if labor can be paid less than its marginal product. Training increases labor's marginal product, and the firm may be able to appropriate some or all of the increase. (2) Profits are also earned from the complementarities between the marginal product of capital and the skills of the labor force. When the quality of the labor force that is operating capital equipment rises, the marginal product of capital rises,[16] yielding higher profits.

Conversely, the marginal product of labor depends on the quality and quantity of capital. Technically a marginal increase in the quantity and quality of one factor does not affect the marginal product of the other factor. In reality changes are never marginal in the technical sense. Increasing the skills of the human labor force raises the returns to both capital and labor, not just to labor, because added human skills significantly alter the stock of labor with which capital works.

---

[16] This can be most clearly seen by differentiating the production function presented in App. A with respect to new capital investment. The marginal product of capital depends on the quantity of labor measured in efficiency units $(L_z(t)^{\lambda}\gamma)$:

$$\frac{\partial Y(t)}{\partial I(t)} = e^{a+bv^2}e^{\alpha t}L_z(t)^{\lambda\gamma}(1 - \lambda)(\gamma)K_x(t)^{[(1-\lambda)(\gamma)-1]}(1 + x)^t$$

The situation facing the private firm is analogous to that facing the private individual, and the equilibrium conditions can be represented in a similar manner:[17]

$$(5\text{-}5) \quad \sum_{i=0}^{n} \frac{MP_0 + (MP_i - W_i) + [(\Delta MP_i^k)(K_i)]}{(1 + r)^n} = \sum_{i=0}^{n} \frac{W_0 + C_i}{(1 + r)^n}$$

where

MP_0 = marginal product of labor before training

MP_i = marginal product of labor after training

W_0 = wage rate of labor before training

W_i = wage rate of labor after training

ΔMP_i^k = change in the marginal product of capital caused by increase in the quality of the labor force

K_i = capital stock

C_i = outlays on training and opportunity costs from training

r = discount rate plus risk premium.

In this model firms invest in training as long as the difference between the marginal product and the wage rate of labor plus the additional returns to capital is greater than the cost of training. The direct returns to a firm from training labor $(MP_i - W_i)$ will be larger (and therefore training most extensive), the more specific the training (W_i will not rise with an increasing MP_i), the greater the monopsony power of the employer (the larger the difference between MP_i and W_i), and the longer the labor contract that can be negotiated (n). The indirect returns from a more profitable capital stock will rise, the greater the size of the capital stock (K_i) and the larger the impact of training on the marginal product of capital (ΔMP_i^k).[18]

[17] This is a modification of Becker's equation. Gary S. Becker, *Human Capital: A Theoretical and Empirical Analysis, with Special Reference to Education* (National Bureau of Economic Research, 1964), p. 20.

[18] Analytically

$$\Delta MP_i^k = \frac{\partial \left(\dfrac{\partial y}{\partial k} \right)}{\partial L_z}$$

where

y = output

k = capital stock

L_z = labor stock in efficiency units to adjust for changes in the quantity of the labor force.

If the costs of training are not homogeneous among individual workers, the distribution as well as absolute amount of human investment by firms is important because of complementarities between formal education and on-the-job training. Training costs may be affected by the amount of human capital already possessed by individual workers. As education rises, the costs of training may fall. If this is the case, costs per worker may differ substantially, and firms will invest in those workers for whom the training costs are lowest. Thus they will choose to train the worker with the largest amount of human capital. Since the poor invest less in their own human capital, private industry will also invest less in them. The result is even greater human capital deficiencies for the poor than those caused by their own investment decisions.

Gary Becker divides training provided by private firms into general and specific.[19] The first is of use to other firms in the economy, while specific training is of use only to the firm actually giving it. Competition for labor insures that the wages of those with general training rise with their marginal productivity, but there is no competitive pressure to insure that wages rise with the marginal productivities of those with specific training. Therefore Becker concludes that individuals must pay for general training[20] and firms must pay for specific training. The group which can appropriate the gains is the one that must make the investment. This conclusion ignores the complementarities between the skills and knowledge of the labor force and the productivity of capital equipment. If training raises the marginal productivity of capital, firms earn profits regardless of whether the training is general or specific. In the same way, there may be complementarities between the two kinds of training. General training may be undertaken because it makes specific training more profitable. Thus the firm may be willing to pay for training even when it cannot appropriate the direct gains. Everything else remaining the same, however, the greater the specificity of training, the greater the profits.

General and specific training are convenient analytic terms, but they actually represent two poles of a continuum. Few types of

[19] Becker, *Human Capital*.
[20] By receiving a wage less than their marginal product.

training are completely specific to one company, and little on-the-job training could really be considered completely general. Firms must decide how far they will move along the continuum between specific and general rather than choose to provide no general and all specific training. In some isolated company towns firms provide all training, including formal elementary and secondary education; in other situations they provide no formal training.

Public policies to increase human investment should be based on a knowledge of what factors influence private firm decisions and how they can be changed in order to increase training investments. Society may wish to encourage the firms to increase such investments. Since on-the-job training is generally given by private firms,[21] the greater the returns from private training, the greater the public interest in increasing private investment in human capital.

As equation (5-5) stands, public policies can affect private manpower decisions only through taxes, subsidies, or wage policies. Profit taxes could be cut to raise the after-tax marginal product stream $\left(\sum_{i=0}^{n} MP_i \right)$; subsidies could be given to hold down the wage stream $\left(\sum_{i=0}^{n} W_i \right)$; or wage policies could be used to hold down the wage stream. The correct course depends on the rationale for public action. There are two options. First, private firms may not know about future or present demands for labor. Individual firms may not be able to see that real or potential shortages exist and that competitive bidding for skilled labor will be self-defeating. Second, to the degree that training is a true externality that cannot be appropriated by the private investor, but accrues to society in the form of higher wages to labor, higher profits to some other business, or lower prices to the consumer, private training decisions will not be optimal. Both reasons lead to a strong case for socially financing training programs, but they do not necessarily lead to public investment. Instead, the criteria of benefit taxation could be used to distribute the cost of training programs. Payments from general revenues should be made only if training is a

[21] Some training is also provided by the military and by the government in its role as an employer.

social goal or merit want. If training programs are designed to achieve society's goals of eliminating poverty, equalizing Negro and white incomes, reducing the minimum level of unemployment, accelerating the rate of growth, or reducing inflationary pressures, general revenues might legitimately be used without violating the general criteria of benefit taxation.

In a static world with perfect labor markets, public influence on private training decisions is limited to the use of taxes, subsidies, and wage controls. The situation is very different, however, in a dynamic world with imperfect labor markets. Such markets of themselves justify more private training. The cost of moving, pension plans, attachment to geographic areas and friends, seniority provision, inadequate knowledge about alternative opportunities, and a host of other factors all lead to a high probability that training returns can be appropriated by the investing firm. General training in effect becomes specific training because of market imperfections.

Everything else being equal, however, firms will always *want* to force the individual to finance the costs of those types of training where the individual makes direct wage gains. One major constraint forcing firms to pay for the costs of general training is the existence of an internal labor market. If the labor market within the firm is separated from the external labor market by constraints on hiring, firing, or promotion, trained workers cannot be hired from the external market. If skilled positions can be filled only by workers already in the internal labor market, firms are forced to provide training, even when trained workers are available in the external labor market or when training is general rather than specific. Most internal labor markets have more than one entry point, but where workers can enter only at the level of the least skilled jobs, firms must internalize the problem of labor training rather than leaving it to the external labor market. The firm may prefer to compel workers to pay for general training, but it cannot exercise this preference if workers must be hired internally.

Firms' ability to force individuals to pay for general training will also depend on the general tightness of the labor market. Unemployment and expectations of future unemployment are impor-

tant determinants of the stream of benefits from training investments, since they indicate the probability that a firm will be able
to hire the desired skills from the pool of unemployed without
having to provide training. Expectation of a 3 percent unemployment rate may lead to very different training decisions from expectations based on a 5 or 6 percent rate. In the latter case, profits can
be earned without the costs of training, since labor skills can be
acquired in the marketplace. In the former case they cannot.

Output expectations are important to training decisions, because they determine the expected demands for skilled workers.
Firms alter their training decisions on the basis of expected needs
and the probabilities of finding the necessary skills in the pool of
unemployed. Long-run private training programs might be very
adequate if everyone's expectations were geared to 3 percent unemployment and the corresponding potential rate of growth. But
training investments might be very inadequate if private expectations were geared to high unemployment rates and long-run unemployment fell without providing private planning time to adjust.

As pointed out above, private firms will provide training to the
worker with the most human capital if private training is complementary to the existing stock of human capital. As unemployment
falls, the stock of human capital possessed by the marginal employee falls, and firms are forced to train those with smaller
amounts of human capital. Thus low unemployment and high
growth can improve the distribution of human investment as well
as its magnitude.

In a dynamic economy, private training expenditures can probably be increased by cutting unemployment to low levels and let-
ting firms, unions, and individuals know that unemployment is
going to be kept there. The firmer this commitment and the more
firmly the private sector is convinced of its validity, the greater the
private training outlays. By committing themselves to low unemployment and high growth, government planners can increase private training. Federal policy makers should seriously consider re-
versing their policies of not setting unemployment goals or giving
firm long-run growth commitments. These commitments do open
the policy maker to charges of failure, since deviations from stated

objectives are easier to spot when the objectives are known; but failing to make public commitments might necessitate an even larger price in inferior private planning and inadequate investment in private training programs.

In addition to improving private information, the government might use public guarantees to encourage private manpower programs. In 1965 the federal government considered guaranteeing the future demand for copper, in order to stimulate the expansion of supplies under conditions where private interests were not sure that additional copper was needed in the long run. Similar guarantees should be considered in order to stimulate the supplies of labor in sectors where differing estimates of future demands for labor block expansion of private training programs. In an area such as construction, where demographic factors indicate a very large boom in the 1960s and 1970s, labor demand guarantees should be seriously considered.

The profitability of training is also a function of the elasticity of substitution between capital and labor. The higher the elasticity, the less training needed. Since substituting capital for skilled labor raises the marginal productivity of unskilled labor, such a substitution can lead to higher wages for unskilled labor. As a means of raising wages for the unskilled in some cases, public research expenditures to speed up the substitution of capital for skilled labor might furnish a viable alternative to large manpower programs.

Training expenditures also depend on the elasticity of substitution of unskilled for skilled labor. Simplifying and dividing jobs so that labor with less training can be used in place of more highly skilled workers is important. Some groups are difficult, if not impossible, to train. For other groups, training probably will not be a profitable investment. Wartime experience, such as that in shipyards, indicates that conscious government policies designed to promote the substitution of unskilled for skilled labor with research and technical assistance might have some effect. The elasticity of substitution for on-the-job skills is also probably affected by the general level of education. The higher the formal level of education, the more flexible the labor force.

Investigations of both individual and firm decisions to invest in human capital indicate that self-interest can lead to a pattern of

human investment that does not further social goals. If public policies cannot indirectly alter the level and distribution of human
capital investments by individuals and private firms, then direct
public investment is necessary. This may take the form of direct
public expenditures or subsidies that are designed to encourage
private training of the disadvantaged. Without this stimulus, private rationality probably will not lead to a satisfactory distribution
of human investment. There seems to be little reason, however,
why a creative use of government policy could not be used to spur
private firms to provide some of the training necessary to reach social objectives, at a lower cost than may be possible with direct
public programs.

DECISIONS BY SOCIETY

Although private individuals do not need to be concerned with
the reasons for connections between education, training, and income flows, society does. Society must determine whether higher
incomes are due to increased output or some other factor. If the
observed relationships between income and education or training
actually represent market imperfections rather than higher productivities, society has two policy options. It may accept the market
imperfections and alter the income distribution by raising education or training levels, or it may choose to alter the income distribution by altering the market imperfections. Methods for doing so
have been outlined. The choice between the two options will depend on the relative costs and benefits. In all probability society
will decide to use both policies.

Implications

Private decisions will not lead to the socially desired distribution
of human capital. Since an optimal income distribution does not
exist, the purchases of human capital must be less than optimal. If
the market for human capital is imperfect and there are social
benefits from human capital investment, the distortions are even
larger. Imperfect knowledge, a less than optimal income distribu-

tion, and imperfections in the capital lending markets all lead to private investment decisions that result in an ever widening distribution of human capital. If public investment in human capital is shortchanging the poor and the racial minorities, the problem is simply compounded. If equalizing the Negro and white income distributions and eliminating the lower tail of the income distribution are important, the distribution of investment in human capital must be altered by public policies.

As will be pointed out in the next chapter, education and on-the-job experience do not completely explain the distribution of earnings, but they are important ingredients. These two factors explain a major proportion of observed income flows. Although the problems of poverty and low Negro incomes cannot be solved by programs to alter either the quantity, quality, or price of human capital, they can be significantly reduced by such programs.

The existence of strong complementarities means that the returns from programs designed to improve education, on-the-job experience, or shift coefficients are heavily dependent on what is happening simultaneously to each of the other variables. Increasing education will have little effect on incomes if individuals work in areas with low shift coefficients and little training. Conversely, education will have a large impact on incomes if the individuals work in areas with ample training and high shift coefficients. The same complementarities affect the returns to programs designed to alter either experience or shift coefficients. If the other factors are unchanged, the returns to any one program will be very low. This means that education programs, training programs, and efforts to move individuals into areas with high shift coefficients must be coordinated. The combination of policies which will produce the greatest income changes at the least cost cannot be determined abstractly. The present positions of the individuals to be aided must be determined. Only then can the marginal benefits and costs be determined.

Given the general characteristics of the poor, large returns could be earned by remedial programs designed to raise everyone in the labor force to at least eighth grade standards of literacy. The social benefits from such a program are large, but from a narrow economic point of view also, the benefits are also large. The marginal income flows from raising education levels in this range are great and the complementarities with on-the-job experience programs are very important. Without this level of education, training has little payoff. Unless an individual possesses an eighth grade literacy standard, he is under a very severe competitive handicap, and as general education levels rise this handicap will grow. Since most individuals in this low range are beyond the normal school age, efforts to bring the working population up to this standard must focus on adult education programs. This is precisely the area where the least effort has been made in educational programs for the poor. Concentrating on children might eliminate poverty in the long run, but the long run is intolerably long. Something must be done for those who are going to be in the labor force for the next thirty years.

For Negroes, however, the principal need is for more on-the-job experience. It is true that education plays a vital role in eliminating the differences between the income distributions for whites and Negroes. Negroes receive less education, and part of the observed differences in the economic returns to education for Negroes is caused by differences in the quality of the education that is provided. Nevertheless, a large fraction of the difference between white and black incomes is explained by differences in the returns to on-the-job experience, from which blacks receive much less value. (See Appendix I for a proposed subsidy system to increase on-the-job experience.) Unless this defect can be corrected, education programs will have little impact on the incomes of blacks in the United States.

CHAPTER VI

The Dispersion of Income

Income is derived from physical capital and human capital, but these are not the only factors determining the distribution of income. Many other influences are at work, because of labor market imperfections.

If labor markets were perfect and completely unchangeable, the supply of and demand for labor with differing skills and knowledge would determine the marginal product of each variety of labor. Individual earnings would equal their marginal products,[1] and the allocation of human capital would determine the distribution of earnings. Labor mobility would insure that persons with the same amount of human capital would receive the same wage rate.[2] Intrinsic ability (the ease of acquiring new skills and knowledge) would influence the distribution of earnings indirectly, since individuals with more ability would find it less costly to acquire human capital and thus would obtain more of it.[3] As a result their incomes would be higher.

The actual distribution of earnings, however, is more disperse than would be predicted from the distribution of education and job experience alone. Labor markets are imperfect and human

---

[1] When there are no economies of scale.

[2] Earnings will be identical only if preferences between leisure and income are identical.

[3] Ability might be broadly defined to include energy, health, and reliability, but these will be assumed to be randomly distributed or constant.

96

capital does not dominate the distribution of earnings in that manner. In reality, there is a wide dispersion of earnings within each class of education and experience. There are many other influential factors—the distribution of monopoly power, economic disequilibria, nonsystematic short-run variations in individual incomes, risk preferences, the distribution of capital-labor ratios and technical progress, lack of labor mobility, and other market imperfections. Monopoly power may raise the wages of some men above their marginal products, while other men may be exploited because of other monopoly powers. Economic disequilibria may lead to wages that are above or below marginal products during transition periods. Nonsystematic random variations in income may harm or benefit a man. With uncertain market conditions, an individual's risk preferences may influence his income. Two men with the same human capital can earn different incomes because they work in industries with different amounts of physical capital and with different levels of technical progress and different capital-labor ratios. In perfect labor markets this could not happen since labor mobility would equalize earnings for those with the same amounts of human capital. All of these market imperfections have a direct impact on the distribution of earnings by eliminating the equality between wages and marginal products. Thus factors other than the distribution of human capital are of major importance in explaining the actual distribution of income.

In Chapter 5 those factors other than education and job experience were lumped together in the shift coefficient of the human capital function, which varied widely across race, region, and occupation. Although the human capital function assumes that all individuals with equal amounts of education and experience receive the average income for that group, there is in reality a wide dispersion of earnings within each class of education and experience.[4] This chapter investigates the other factors that may explain some of this dispersion (except for racial prejudice, which is discussed in the next chapter).

[4] Entrepreneurial ability is counted as part of human capital and acquired through experience.

The Impact of Human Capital

By using the human capital function developed in Chapter 5 and inserting into it the actual cross-distributions of education and experience for Negroes and whites (see Appendix J), it is possible to calculate for each group a hypothetical income distribution based solely on the allocation of human capital. One can then compare the hypothetical with the actual distribution of income; there are great differences between them.

Table 6-1 shows that in 1959 for men between the ages of eighteen and sixty-four the hypothetical income distribution was much less disperse than the actual.[5] Whites with incomes below $2,000 or above $6,000 were hypothetically only 20.1 percent of the total, but the actual figure was 49.4. Nonwhites having incomes below $1,000 or above $4,000 showed a hypothetical 7.1 percent but an actual 47.9 percent. The actual income distribution would be much more equal than it is if the distribution of human capital were the only factor involved. Instead of 8.8 million men with incomes of less than $2,000, there would be only 3.8 million.

The human capital function implicitly assumes the existence of perfect labor markets[6]—an assumption embedded in the shift coefficient, which is considered to be the same for each individual by race and region. Other than his human capital, the same external factors are assumed to affect his income.

Since the hypothetical distribution of income differs from the actual, this assumption of constant shift coefficients in the human capital function is false. External factors have different impacts on individuals. Persons with the same human capital are working with different shift coefficients. Those coefficients must differ systematically by income class to duplicate the actual in-

[5] Since males aged eighteen to sixty-four earn approximately 80 percent of total earnings and dominate the national income distribution, ignoring females, young workers, and elderly workers does not present a serious problem. U.S. Bureau of the Census, *U.S. Census of Population: 1960*, Vol. 1, *Characteristics of the Population*, Pt. 1, *United States Summary* (1964), pp. 553, 555.

[6] The same differences emerge when the human capital function is applied to earnings data rather than income data. Income data are used here since they are available for whites and Negroes with more human capital cells than earnings data.

TABLE 6-1

Actual and Hypothetical Distribution of Income for Males
Aged Eighteen to Sixty-four, United States, 1959

(In percentages)

Income class (Thousands of dollars)	Distribution among whites			Distribution among nonwhites		
	Actual income	Hypo-thetical income	Actual earnings	Actual income	Hypo-thetical income	Actual earnings
0– 1	8.3	0.5	6.2	20.8	1.4	17.8
1– 2	8.7	5.9	7.1	17.4	24.0	16.2
2– 3	9.2	9.5	9.0	18.7	47.7	19.6
3– 4	11.9	26.8	12.4	16.0	21.2	17.3
4– 5	14.3	25.7	15.4	12.6	3.8	13.9
5– 6	15.2	17.9	16.5	8.0	.9	8.8
6– 7	10.7	2.5	11.4	3.2	1.0	3.3
7–10	13.6	9.7	14.0	2.5	0.0	2.4
10–15	5.0	1.5	5.0	0.5	0.0	0.5
15 and over	3.1	0.0	3.0	0.3	0.0	0.3
Total	100.0	100.0	100.0	100.0	100.0	100.0

Sources: Actual income data are from U.S. Bureau of the Census, *U.S. Census of Population: 1960, Educational Attainment*, Final Report PC(2)-5B (1963), pp. 88–91. The hypothetical income distribution is based on the actual distribution of human capital; see discussion in the text. Earnings data are from *U.S. Census of Population: 1960, Occupation by Earnings and Education*, Final Report PC(2)-7B (1963), pp. 2, 3, 244. Figures are rounded and will not necessarily add to totals.

come distribution. Those with low incomes on average work with lower shift coefficients than those with high incomes. Thus the dispersion of shift coefficients necessary to explain the actual distribution of income represents the impact of factors other than human capital.

There are, however, a large number of cross-distributions of shift coefficients and human capital which could explain the actual income distribution. Perhaps the most interesting is that distribution of coefficients that with minimum dispersion would reproduce the actual income distribution. The actual dispersion of shift coefficients may be greater than the minimum, but the latter at least places a lower bound on the influence of factors other than human capital. Their influence cannot be less extensive though it may be more so.

The minimum dispersion of shift coefficients is calculated by assuming that they are distributed in the same manner as human capital. Where human capital is low, they are low. Where human capital is high, they are high. Thus shift coefficients and the distribution of human capital complement each other in determining incomes and do not work at cross purposes. If a larger number of workers is needed in the lowest income class of the hypothetical income distribution to equalize the hypothetical with the actual, the shift coefficients of the workers in the income class immediately above are lowered to move individuals from that class into the lowest class (see Appendix J for the detailed calculations). Lowering the shift coefficients for those with more human capital reduces their incomes. Given the amount that shift coefficients must be lowered to balance the hypothetical number of workers in the lowest income class with the actual, an average shift coefficient can be calculated for those workers.

The shift coefficients in the human capital functions in Chapter 5 were $783 for Negroes and $1,140 for whites (Table 5-1). To reproduce the actual income distribution, the shift coefficients for whites must range from an average of $359 in the $0–$1,000 income class to $1,854 in the $15,000 and up class (see Table 6-2). The corresponding range for Negroes is from $282 to $2,407.

The impact of market imperfections is not randomly distributed across income classes, but varies systematically. Those at the bottom of the income distribution are adversely affected by market imperfections and those at the top are beneficially affected.

Factors Leading to Dispersion

Other elements in income distribution, some of which have been mentioned above, may now be examined in more detail.

WEALTH

The distribution of income is slightly more disperse than that of earnings since wealth is more inequitably distributed, but the differences are not great. The actual distribution of earnings is very similar to the actual distribution of income (see Table 6-1). It was pointed out above that in 1959 among males aged eighteen to sixty-four 49.4 percent of the whites had incomes below $2,000 or over $6,000 and 47.9 percent of the nonwhites had incomes under $1,000 or above $4,000. The corresponding figures for earnings were 46.7 percent of whites and 47.0 percent of nonwhites. The greatest differences occurred in the $0–$1,000 income class— 2.1 percentage points for whites, 3.0 for nonwhites. Thus the distribution of wealth explains very little of the difference between the actual and the hypothetical distribution of income.

TABLE 6-2

Minimum Dispersion in Shift Coefficients Necessary to Reproduce the Actual Distribution of Income for Males Aged Eighteen to Sixty-four, United States, 1959

Income class (Thousands of dollars)	Shift coefficient	
	White	Nonwhite
0– 1	$ 359	$ 282
1– 2	649	538
2– 3	814	786
3– 4	1,140	1,096
4– 5	1,220	1,011
5– 6	1,388	1,229
6– 7	1,347	1,197
7–10	1,481	1,334
10–15	1,676	1,506
15 and over[a]	1,854	2,407

Source: Author's estimates. See App. J.
a. Average income for this class is assumed to be $20,000.

ABILITY

As previously mentioned, ability affects the distribution of income through its impact on the distribution of human capital. Those with greater ability may invest more in their human capital because the economic returns are expected to be larger. If ability and human capital are complementary, some of the impact of ability has already been considered in the human capital function. Some of the returns attributed to education should properly be attributed to ability. This leads to errors in estimating the marginal product of education, but the hypothetical distribution of income generated with the human capital function is determined partly by the distribution of ability as a result. If education and ability were perfectly correlated, the impact of ability would have been completely considered.

In imperfect and uncertain labor markets, with complementarities between ability, existing skills, and the ease with which new skills can be learned, ability may add to income by increasing a worker's potential flexibility. Two workers may possess the same quantity of human capital, but one of them may be more valuable since he can be more easily trained for a new job.

If ability is taken to mean that which is measured by intelligence quotient (IQ) scores, it probably does not alter the dispersion of income very much beyond that already included in the human capital function. IQs are assumed to be much less disperse than incomes, with 90 percent of the population within 22.5 percentage points of the median intelligence quotient.[7] In the case of incomes of males between eighteen and sixty-four, only 33 percent of the whites are within this same range of the median white income and 24 percent of nonwhites in the range of nonwhite income.[8] Even assuming that low abilities are concentrated among those with little human capital and high abilities among those with an abundance does not add much to the predicted dispersion of incomes. When ability is more broadly defined to include entrepreneurial capacity, creativity, personal habits, and the energy for physical as well as mental tasks, it probably contributes much more to the observed dispersion of income. However, it is then much less intrinsic and becomes a factor that can be altered by environment and training.

TECHNICAL PROGRESS AND CAPITAL-LABOR RATIOS

In periods of disequilibrium, or if labor markets were relatively imperfect across industries but relatively perfect within industries,

---

[7] David Wechsler, *Wechsler Adult Intelligence Scale Manual* (Psychological Corp., 1955), p. 20.

[8] U.S. Bureau of the Census, *U.S. Census of Population: 1960, Occupation by Earnings and Education*, pp. 2, 3, 244.

workers might be paid according to their marginal productivities; but the marginal productivity of different types of labor may not be equalized across industries. In this situation the distribution of technical progress and of capital-labor ratios would have a major impact on the distribution of income. Wages for workers with the same quantity of human capital would depend on their particular industry or profession. Those who worked under conditions of high capital-labor ratios and advanced technologies would have large incomes; those who worked with low capital-labor ratios and backward technologies would have low incomes.

Capital-labor ratios and technical progress seem to be widely dispersed among sectors of the economy. The average manufacturing corporation in the first quarter of 1967 held capital assets of $21,741 per employee, but industry means ranged from $419,212 for petroleum refining to $5,396 for apparel (see Table 6-3). Value added per employee shows similar variations: by region the range in 1962 was from $9,134 in New England to $11,853 in the East North Central region, by industry from $5,783 in apparel to $22,291 in petroleum (see Table 6-4). If the capital-labor ratios and value added per employee were known for firms or for industries outside the manufacturing sector, the range of variation would be even greater. There is sufficient variation both in technical progress and capital-labor ratios to have a sizable impact on the distribution of income.

With labor market imperfections of this nature, individual earnings depend on the cross-distributions of human capital, physical capital, and technical progress. Although there are no direct estimates of the relevant cross-distributions, indirect estimates can be made by combining the human capital function with the production functions.

Production functions and the human capital function are closely related. Production functions examine the marginal productivity of the average worker. The human capital function examines the marginal productivity of labor across various human capital classes; it stresses the impact of education and experience on productivity under the assumption that all other factors that might affect incomes are constant or randomly distributed across income classes. The production function allows technical progress and

TABLE 6-3

Capital Assets per Employee in Manufacturing, by Industry,
United States, First Quarter 1967

(*In dollars*)

Industry	Assets per employee	Industry	Assets per employee
All manufacturing		Miscellaneous manufacturing,	
corporations	*21,741*	and ordnance	7,725
Transportation equipment	24,884	Food and kindred products	20,267
Motor vehicles and		Dairy products	18,796
equipment	37,117	Bakery products	6,690
Aircraft and parts	16,223	Tobacco manufactures	56,110
Electrical machinery, equip-		Textile mill products	12,535
ment, and supplies	17,137	Apparel and related products	5,396
Other machinery	19,178	Paper and allied products	21,243
Metalworking machinery	13,000	Printing and publishing,	
Other fabricated metal		except newspapers	12,080
products	12,945	Chemicals and allied products	42,064
Primary metal industries	30,182	Drugs	46,280
Stone, clay, and glass		Petroleum refining and	
products	20,621	related industries	347,607
Furniture and fixtures	7,383	Petroleum refining	419,212
Lumber and wood products	11,836	Rubber and miscellaneous	
Instruments and related		plastic products	17,854
products	19,190	Leather and leather products	7,966

Sources: U.S. Federal Trade Commission-Securities and Exchange Commission, *Quarterly Financial Report for Manufacturing Corporations, First Quarter 1967* (1967), pp. 34–49, and U.S. Bureau of Labor Statistics, *Employment and Earnings and Monthly Report on the Labor Force*, Vol. 13 (April 1967), pp. 34–38.

physical capital to vary. In the human capital function the shift coefficients represent the impact of the physical capital and technical progress in the production function.[9] When capital-labor ratios and technical progress rise, the shift coefficient rises; when they fall, the shift coefficient falls.

The marginal product of individual workers depends on their human capital, their personal capital-labor ratio, and the technical efficiency of the organization in which they work—the same factors as for labor collectively.[10] Ideally these three elements could be in-

[9] If the human capital function were used to explain incomes over time, the shift coefficient would have to change from year to year to account for changes in the level of technical progress and capital-labor ratios.

[10] The marginal product of individual workers would technically be determined by finding the marginal product of their marginal hour of work.

TABLE 6-4

Value Added per Employee in Manufacturing,
by Region and Industry, United States, 1962

(*In dollars*)

Category	Value added per employee
Region	
United States	11,093
New England	9,134
Middle Atlantic	10,132
East North Central	11,853
West North Central	11,227
South Atlantic	9,476
East South Central	9,603
West South Central	11,657
Mountain	11,540
Pacific	11,610
Industry	
Food and kindred products	12,398
Tobacco products	21,274
Textile mill products	6,942
Apparel and related products	5,783
Lumber and wood products	6,560
Furniture and fixtures	7,728
Paper and allied products	12,152
Printing and publishing	10,807
Chemicals and allied products	22,080
Petroleum and coal products	22,291
Rubber and plastics products	10,841
Leather and leather products	6,082
Stone, clay, and glass products	11,508
Primary metal industries	12,129
Fabricated metal products	10,252
Machinery, except electrical	11,088
Electrical machinery	10,659
Transportation equipment	13,142
Instruments and related products	11,339

Source: U.S. Bureau of the Census, *Annual Survey of Manufactures: 1962* (1964), pp. 16, 18–26.

serted into a production function to calculate a distribution of labor's marginal product.

Since the data do not exist for individual production functions, this method cannot be used. A step can be taken in this direction, however, by combining the production function with the human capital function, which has already been used to calculate the dispersion of shift coefficients necessary to duplicate the actual distribution of income. Under the asumption that workers are paid their marginal products but marginal products are not equalized across industries, the dispersion in shift coefficients is caused by a dispersion in the distributions of capital-labor ratios and technical progress. By using the production function results, it is possible to calculate the distribution of capital-labor ratios and technical progress that would be necessary to explain the estimated dispersion of shift coefficients. As pointed out earlier, those with low incomes work in industries and occupations with low capital-labor ratios and low levels of technical progress. Those with high incomes work with high capital-labor ratios and high levels of technical progress.

A large number of cross-distributions of capital-labor ratios and technical progress could explain the distribution of shift coefficients. As with the calculation of the dispersion of shift coefficients, the minimum dispersion hypothesis will be used. Thus the lower bound of possible dispersions is being calculated. Since capital-labor ratios and technical progress both lead to higher incomes, they are assumed to be distributed together in a manner which leads to the least dispersion of each. Each is assumed to explain 50 percent of the necessary dispersion of shift coefficients.[11] Under these assumptions capital-labor ratios for nonwhites ranged from $186 in the lowest income class to $104,000 in the highest income class in 1959 (Table 6-5). For whites the range was from $385 to $42,100. Indexes of technical progress ranged from 49 to 145 for nonwhites and from 56 to 130 for whites. The wider dispersion for Negroes is easily explained if the extent of discrimination differs by income class. Negro shift coefficients would be dispersed because of discrimination as well as capital-labor ratios and technical progress. Different assumptions about the division of responsibility between capital-labor ratios and technical progress would produce different results, but the changes would be offsetting. A smaller range of capital-labor ratios necessitates a larger range for the index of technical progress and vice versa.

[11] There is no strong reason for picking 50 percent rather than some other assumption. Fifty percent was chosen since disembodied technical progress and the capital stock had similar effects on the marginal product of labor from 1929 to 1965 (see Chap. 3).

TABLE 6-5

Capital-Labor Ratios and Indexes of Technical Progress,
by Income Class, United States, 1959

Income class (Thousands of dollars)	Capital-labor ratio		Index of technical progress[a]	
	Nonwhite	White	Nonwhite	White
0– 1	$ 186	$ 385	49	56
1– 2	1,260	2,194	69	76
2– 3	3,810	4,283	83	85
3– 4	10,253	11,489	98	100
4– 5	8,080	14,036	94	103
5– 6	14,400	20,500	104	110
6– 7	13,300	18,800	102	109
7–10	18,300	24,821	108	114
10–15	26,100	35,700	115	121
15 and over	104,000	42,100	145	130

Source: Author's estimates. See discussion in text.
a. White $3,000–$4,000 income class = 100.

In reality the dispersion of capital-labor ratios and technical progress does not completely explain the dispersion of income. The calculations are only meant to be illustrative of the kind of results that emerge from this hypothesis. The reader can easily make his own assumption about the importance of failing to equalize marginal products across industries and scale the results down accordingly. I do not know of any method to determine the precise impact.

MONOPOLY OR MONOPSONY POWER

If there are systematic differences in the monopoly or monopsony power of capital and labor across income classes, this may contribute to the actual dispersion of income. Income may be more widely dispersed than human capital if the bargaining power of labor vis-à-vis capital becomes weaker the less human capital that is possessed. Those with little human capital may be paid relatively less of their marginal product than those with more human capital. As yet, there is no method to determine whether the differences between wages and marginal productivities vary systematically by income class.[12]

To estimate the importance of relative bargaining power, a comparison of the distributions of income and the distribution of marginal products would have to be made after allowing for the impact of physical capital and technical progress. Unfortunately the data do not exist to make such a calculation. Absence of data, however, does not mean that relative bargaining power is unimportant. If systematic differences in relative bargaining power are important, the dispersion of capital-labor ratios and technical progress would be less than that indicated in Table 6-5. Some of the actual dispersion of income would be accounted for by bargaining power. In reality bargaining power probably plays a role in the actual distribution of income.

RISK PREFERENCES AND SHORT-RUN INCOME VARIABILITY

In an uncertain world incomes will be dispersed since different individuals have different expectations about future events and different risk preferences. Some enjoy risky situations; others do not. Those who accurately predict future events and are willing to undertake risks receive higher incomes; those who do not accurately predict future events or who are not willing to undertake risks receive lower incomes. Since most incomes are not earned in entrepreneurial activities, however, risk preferences and forecasting abilities are not likely to explain the wide dispersion of wage and salary increases.

Random short-run factors, good or bad luck, affect the incomes of many families, but they do not dominate the annual income distribution. The distribution of lifetime incomes probably looks very similar to the distribution of annual incomes. Evidence is scanty, but the indication from available data is that individuals occupy relatively stable positions in the income distribution, espe-

[12] A priori it would be expected that those with high incomes are paid at or above their marginal products while those wth low incomes are paid less than their marginal products.

cially males in the eighteen to sixty-four age bracket. Most of those families in poverty in any one year are in poverty in the next year or very close to it. There are large gross flows up and down the income distribution, but they cancel out over very short periods of time. The Council of Economic Advisers concludes that statistics suggesting that about 20 percent of the poverty-stricken families in any given year are no longer poor in the following year certainly over-state the degree of real improvement in the income position of this group. They fail to reveal the extent to which many of these families hover about the $3,000 income line. An increase in income from $2,900 to $3,100 hardly constitutes an escape from poverty and, furthermore, may be quickly reversed. Therefore, some measure of poverty covering more than a one-year period is more appropriate and useful in identifying the incidence of chronic poverty. A poverty criterion based on a two-year income average of $3,000 yields nearly as many low-income families as is indicated by the one-year measure.[13]

Conclusions

The distribution of human capital is an important ingredient in the distribution of income, but it is not the sole ingredient. The actual dispersion of income is much greater than would be predicted by the distribution of human capital. The distributions of physical wealth, ability, technical progress, capital-labor ratios, monopoly powers, and risk preferences lead to a dispersed distribution of income.

Programs to eliminate poverty and economic discrimination have concentrated on improving the distribution of human capital. Such programs may be necessary, but they are not the only manner in which the income distribution can be narrowed. Many of the factors leading to a dispersed income distribution can be reduced if not eliminated by improving labor or industrial mobility.[14] If labor mobility can be improved, market imperfections will be less and this will reduce the impact of capital-labor ratios and technical progress on earnings. Specific industry or occupation capital-labor

[13] *Economic Report of the President, January 1965,* p. 165.
[14] Labor mobility can be created by moving workers to jobs or moving jobs to workers.

ratios or levels of technical progress would become much less important to the distribution of earnings. The distribution of earnings in a perfect labor market would more closely resemble the distribution of human capital. By itself this would result in a much narrower distribution of income. Further narrowing of the income distribution would then require narrowing the distribution of human capital.

Equalizing the distributions of white and Negro incomes presents a very similar set of problems. Factors other than the distribution of human capital explain many of the observed differences. In addition to improving labor mobility and increasing human capital, eliminating the handicap of discrimination is important. Negroes have less human capital and receive less remuneration for what human capital they have, but they also suffer from a much more adverse distribution of market imperfections. Racial prejudice and discrimination are undoubtedly an important element of the greater market imperfections facing Negroes. Without eliminating discrimination, Negro poverty cannot be eliminated and the Negro and white income distributions cannot be equalized.

CHAPTER VII

Discrimination

In the preceding chapters conditions facing Negroes have been shown to be fundamentally different from those facing whites. Negro income distribution lags approximately thirty years behind. The sheer fact of being black explains 38 percent of the difference in the incidence of poverty for whites and Negroes. Better utilization of economic resources improves job and income opportunities of Negroes, but after adjustment for cyclical effects there have been no favorable (or unfavorable) trends in those opportunities in the postwar period. Even at very high utilization levels, median Negro family incomes remain at only 60 percent of white family incomes.[1] Smaller amounts of human capital prove to have a marked impact on the incomes of Negroes, who not only receive less education and training than whites but also obtain lower returns from them. Moreover, Negroes work in industries and occupations with significantly less physical capital and technical progress. All of these items reflect discrimination, but these factors alone do not account for Negro income levels. Something further remains to be explained.

Discrimination is important not only because it produces low incomes: it also diminishes the effectiveness of many of the instruments used in fighting poverty. If discrimination reduces Negro returns to education, for instance, education may be a poor weapon

[1] U.S. Bureau of the Census, *Current Population Reports*, Series P-23, No. 26, BLS Report 347, "Recent Trends in Social and Economic Conditions of Negroes in the United States" (1968), p. 6.

to reduce Negro poverty although excellent for reducing white poverty.

To understand how discrimination causes low Negro incomes, it is necessary to understand how it operates. How were the effects outlined above produced? What actions do whites take when they discriminate? What are the economic costs of discrimination? What must the government do to eliminate it?

These questions cannot be answered theoretically. To design a strategy for eliminating discrimination, the magnitudes of different types of discrimination must be known. To provide empirical estimates, the theory of discrimination is applied to actual data in order to calculate Negro losses and white gains from different types of discrimination, and the social costs. Analysis in previous chapters has centered on Negro economic losses. To emphasize the reverse side of the discrimination problem, this chapter focuses on white gains; but it should be remembered in either case that a white gain corresponds to a Negro loss and vice versa.

The Existing Theory

Current knowledge about the theory of discrimination rests almost entirely on the work of Gary Becker.[2] In his analysis, discrimination is a restrictive practice that interrupts free trade between two independent societies, white and Negro. If free trade existed, the Negro society would export labor (its relatively abundant factor of production) and the white society would export capital (its relatively abundant factor) until the marginal products of labor and capital were equal in both societies. This would come about because each individual is maximizing a utility function which has income as its single argument.

However, when there is discrimination, individuals in the white society maximize a utility function which has both income and physical distance from Negroes as arguments. Whites are willing to pay a premium not to associate with Negroes; as a result they import less Negro labor and export less white capital. Since discrimi-

[2] Gary S. Becker, *The Economics of Discrimination* (University of Chicago Press, 1957).

nation holds trade below free trade levels, not only does total output fall, but the output of both communities falls because of the
inefficient distribution of economic resources. The returns to
white labor and Negro capital rise, but these are more than offset
by declining returns to white capital and Negro labor.

The central proposition following from this theory is that
"when actual discrimination occurs, he [the discriminator] must, in
fact, either pay or forfeit income for this privilege."[3] In other
words, the discriminator must lose income if he wishes to discriminate. If this deduction is correct, empirical impressions are amaz-
ingly false. Do the whites of South Africa or the United States
really have lower standards of living as a result of their discrimination? If they do, increases in those standards can be used as an inducement to persuade them to give up their prejudices against
Negroes. Eliminating discrimination in this case is certainly easier
than in the case where it results in reductions in white standards of
living.

Becker's "discrimination coefficient" (DC) corresponds to a
tariff in international trade. "Suppose an *employer* were faced
with the money wage rate π of a particular factor; he is assumed to
act as if π $(1 + d_i)$ were the *net* wage rate, with d_i as his DC against
this factor."[4] The discrimination coefficient is a method of representing a downward shift in the white demand curve for Negro
labor. The vertical shift represents the size of the coefficient, on
which depends the effect that the downward shift will have on
Negro and white incomes, but that effect also depends on the supply
elasticity of Negro labor and the white demand elasticity for Negro
labor, as shown in Figure 7-1.

If the elasticity of supply (S) is zero (first panel), Negro wages
(W) decline with a downward shift in demand from D_1 to D_2, but
the quantity of Negro labor (Q) is constant. The return to the
white community must rise since Negro wages are now less than
their marginal product. In this panel white gains are equal to the
rectangle $ABCD$. If the elasticity of supply is infinite (second panel),
wages are constant and all of the adjustment occurs in the quantity
of labor supplied. The white community loses the intermarginal

[3] *Ibid.*, p. 6.
[4] *Ibid.*

FIGURE 7-1

White Gains and Losses from Discrimination

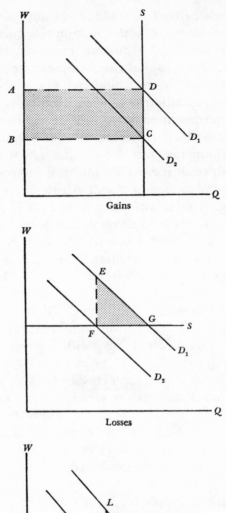

Gains

Losses

Gains and losses

See text for explanatory remarks.

114

product (producer's surplus) *EFG;* no gains are possible, since Negroes cannot be paid less than their marginal product. If the elasticity of supply is greater than zero but less than infinite (third panel), both gains and losses occur. The net gain or loss depends on the relative size of *HIJK* and *LKM.*[5]

Not only can whites gain from discrimination, but previous work has shown how to determine optimum tariffs (discrimination coefficients).[6] These studies have much stronger implications for discrimination than simply pointing out that the discriminator may benefit. The discriminator may gain in the face of retaliation or the retaliator may be able to improve on his free trade position in the face of discrimination.[7]

[5] More precisely:

(A)
$$\Delta P(N_0 - \Delta N) \geq < \tfrac{1}{2}N(DP_0 - \Delta P)$$

where

ΔP = change in the price of Negro labor
N_0 = initial quantity of Negro labor exported
ΔN = change in the quantity of Negro labor exported
N = Negro labor
D = discrimination coefficient
P_0 = initial price of Negro labor.

Substituting the relevant demand and supply elasticities into (A) yields

(B)
$$\frac{De_0P_0}{e_s + e_d}\left[N_0 - \frac{N_0De_se_d}{e_s + e_d}\right] \geq < \tfrac{1}{2}\frac{N_0e_se_dD}{e_s + e_d}\left[DP_0 - \frac{De_0P_0}{e_s + e_d}\right]$$

or

(C)
$$1 - \frac{De_se_d}{2e_s + e_d} \geq < \frac{e_sD}{2}$$

where

e_d = white elasticity of demand for Negro labor
e_s = supply elasticity for Negro labor.

When $e_s = 0$, white losses are zero and when $e_s = \infty$, white gains are zero. Generally white losses do not exceed white gains unless both e_s and e_d are large.

[6] Harry G. Johnson, "Optimum Tariffs and Retaliation," *International Trade and Economic Growth* (George Allen & Unwin, Ltd., 1958), p. 31.

[7] *Ibid.*, p. 35 ff., for a proof of this proposition. Johnson finds that the discriminator (retaliator) benefits even in the face of retaliation (discrimination) when his elasticity of demand for imports is roughly more than two and one-half times as large as the elasticity of demand of the retaliator (discriminator). When the elasticities of demand are approximately equal, both countries lose, and between there is a range of indeterminacy.

For a formal application of these principles to Becker's model, see Anne O. Krueger, "The Economics of Discrimination," *Journal of Political Economy*, Vol. 71 (October 1963), pp. 481–86.

For Becker, the possibility of white monetary gains merely represents payment for the nonmonetary costs of production[8] (disutility) of having to associate with Negroes. The extra white incomes represent real psychological costs of production and not net returns. Three points should be established: (1) The additional output accrues to the white community and expands its consumption possibility schedule. (2) Using net utility rather than gross income is acceptable as long as everyone understands the unit of measurement. If net gains and losses are being examined, all other disutilities of production must also be subtracted from gross monetary incomes. Since labor is supplied to the point where the marginal disutility of giving up leisure and the disutilities of production (such as physical discomfort and monotony) are equal to the wage rate, the marginal return to labor or any other factor of production must be zero. If the marginal return were greater than zero, more labor would be supplied until wage rate reductions brought the marginal return back to zero. Introducing discrimination coefficients into a system of production means simply that the marginal disutility of supplying factors of production increases and that the supplies of these factors of production will be correspondingly reduced. (3) If racial prejudice already exists among whites but they have not been able to act upon it, introducing discrimination can give them a clear gain in net utilities. Real incomes can increase in the manner outlined above, and reducing the number of Negroes with whom whites are forced to associate results in higher utility from the physical distance argument of the utility function. Fewer Negroes means less disutility from associating with them. The result is a clear white gain in net utility.

Only if white economic incomes do not increase and if racial prejudices suddenly emerge at the instant discrimination is put into practice must whites' net utility fall. If only one of these conditions exists, empirical information is necessary to determine whether whites gain or lose.

[8] Becker, *Economics of Discrimination*, p. 7.

An Alternative Theory

Applying the theory of tariffs to a world of perfect competition has serious limitations in a world where much of the impact of discrimination comes from the monopoly powers of the discriminator rather than from his inability to distort perfect competition with trade barriers. Some types of discrimination seem to fit Becker's model but many do not. Discrimination cannot be represented adequately by a model of two independent societies freely trading with each other over the barriers created by economic discrimination. Racial discrimination occurs in one society, not two. The dominant group controls much more than its willingness to trade or not to trade with the minority group. Physical, social, or economic pressures may enable the dominant group to trade with the subservient group as a discriminating monopolist or monopsonist. The minority group may have few options and certainly not the option of refusing to trade. Subsistence (social or physical) may require trade. Negroes live in a white supremacist society, not just a segregated society.

Discrimination is not simply demanding a premium to associate with Negroes, as described by Becker.[9] The discriminator may want to work with, buy from, or hire Negroes, but he insists on specifying the relationships under which the two parties will meet and how the Negro will respond. Perhaps it is more accurate to say that whites maximize a utility function with social distance rather than physical distance as one of its arguments. A desire for social distance can lead to a very different set of actions. The discriminator may prefer to hire Negro maids, Negro garbage collectors, or to work with Negroes if he can be in a position of authority. He may also prefer to hire Negro labor if it can be exploited to increase his own profits.

Varieties of Discrimination

A long list of types of discrimination could be compiled, but most can be subsumed under seven general categories: (1) employment

[9] *Ibid.*

(unemployment, both full-time and part-time, is concentrated among Negroes); (2) wages (Negroes are simply paid less for the same work); (3) occupation (quantitative controls limit or prevent Negro entry into some occupations, and supplies of Negro labor to the unrestricted occupations are correspondingly enlarged); (4) human capital (less is invested in human capital for Negroes than for whites); (5) capital (price discrimination and/or quantitative controls limit Negroes' ability to borrow from the capital markets, or the rate of return on Negro capital can be lowered by a variety of techniques); (6) monopoly power (Negro factors of production are not permitted to enter those areas where monopolies result in factor returns above those prevailing in a competitive economy); (7) price (Negro buyers are required to pay above market prices and Negro sellers must sell at below market prices).

These seven types are discussed in this section under the assumption that a rational discriminator (for example, a monopolist named "whites") is trying to maximize his gains from discrimination, including economic gains and increases in social distance. This procedure does not imply that the assumption is correct; it simply permits us to determine whether white gains are possible and to view the causes of the gains or losses. Additionally it focuses attention on the clashes between different types of discrimination. Maximizing the gains from one type of discrimination may clash with maximizing the gains from another type. Conflicts between different discriminators represent one of the major problems faced by them as a group. To solve these conflicts, anomalies often seem to appear in the observed pattern of discrimination.

EMPLOYMENT

This type of discrimination results in gains for whites without any offsetting losses.[10] If Negroes suffer more than their proportionate share of unemployment, the number of employed whites increases and their incomes are larger than they would be otherwise.

[10] This refers simply to private monetary gains and does not include social costs such as the slums produced by Negro poverty.

To maximize white gains from employment discrimination, Negroes should be distributed across occupations, industries, and geographic areas in such a way that their employment is equal to the maximum expected unemployment in each category and they can be forced to bear the entire burden of unemployment in each. If the total Negro labor force is not as large as the maximum expected unemployment, efficient employment discrimination will dictate that Negro employment should be concentrated in high-wage areas since the greatest gains can be made by substituting whites for Negroes there. White unemployment would be allowed only in the lowest paying occupations. The employment distribution which attempts to maximize white gains from employment discrimination will obviously conflict with attempts to maximize gains from occupational discrimination. Employment discrimination may call for employment of Negroes in high-wage occupations, while occupational discrimination calls for employment of Negroes in low-wage occupations.

WAGES

If wage discrimination and quantitative controls over Negro employment are possible, white incomes can be enlarged by distributing Negro employment optimally (from the standpoint of resource allocation) throughout the occupational structure and thereupon appropriating part of each Negro's marginal product by paying him less than his product. If the distribution of white employment and capital is independent of the distribution of Negro employment, the discriminator will want to maximize the difference between Negro marginal products and Negro wages.[11] If the marginal products of Negro laborers are not affected by incentives, white incomes would be maximized by paying subsistence wages to

---

[11] The discriminator would want to maximize the following expression:

$$\sum_{i=1}^{n} [(MP_{Li}^{N} - W_{i}^{N})(E_{i}^{N})]$$

where
  MP_{Li}^{N} = marginal product of Negro labor in occupation i
  W_{i}^{N} = wages of Negro labor in occupation i
  E_{i}^{N} = supply of Negro labor in occupation i.

Negroes and using quantitative controls to distribute their employment in such a way as to equalize the difference between marginal
products and wages in each occupation. If Negro marginal products depend on incentives, wages should be set in each occupation
to maximize the difference between the marginal product and the
wage rate; quantitative employment controls could then equalize
the differences across occupations. In either case white incomes are
clearly larger as a result of discrimination. Whites have been able
to appropriate part of the marginal product of Negro labor and
there have been no losses from an inefficient distribution of economic resources.

If the distribution of white employment and capital is not independent of the distribution of Negro employment, the net gains or
losses will depend on whether the gains from appropriating part of
the Negro marginal product are greater than the losses from the
inefficient distribution of white labor and capital.[12] Whether gains
or losses occur depends on the supply price elasticities for white
labor and capital and the elasticities of the marginal products of
capital and labor with respect to changes in the quantities of each
employed. If white labor and capital supply curves are inelastic, if
the marginal product curves are inelastic, and if wage discrimination is extensive, whites probably gain. With these conditions,
there is little distortion in the distribution of capital and labor,
and the gains from discrimination are large.

In a different case, with wage discrimination but no quantitative
controls over Negro employment, the analysis is very similar. Instead of considering only the effects of wages on work incentives

[12] Analytically, are the gains on the left side of the following expression greater
or less than the losses on the right side?

$$\sum_{i=1}^{n} (MP_{Li}^{N} - W_i^{N})E_i^{N} \geq\; < \sum_{i=1}^{n} (K_i^{w})(\Delta MP_{Ki}^{w}) + \sum_{i=1}^{n} (E_i^{w})(\Delta MP_{Li}^{w})$$

where

MP_{Li}^{N} = marginal product of Negro labor in occupation i
W_i^{N} = wages of Negro labor in occupation i
E_i^{N} = supply of Negro labor in occupation i
K_i^{w} = supply of white capital in occupation i
ΔMP_{Ki}^{w} = change in the marginal product of white capital in occupation i
E_i^{w} = supply of white labor in occupation i
ΔMP_{Li}^{w} = change in the marginal product of white labor in occupation i.

within an occupation, the effect of wages on supplies of Negro labor to an occupation must also be taken into account. The lower the elasticity of the Negro labor supply curve, the larger are white gains from discrimination. With inelastic Negro labor supply curves, wage discrimination can be undertaken without causing large distortions in the supplies of Negro labor.

OCCUPATION

Here white income gains result from creating a white occupational distribution weighted toward high-wage occupations. Incomes are higher than they would be if whites were efficiently (on the basis of resource allocation) distributed across occupations. White costs are those of the extra investment necessary to train less talented whites for skilled occupations, or the losses to white capital or labor from having less qualified individuals in the occupations.[13]

The white community may lose from wage and occupational discrimination, but this is not to say that the actual discriminator within the white community also loses by practicing discrimination. Discrimination may produce inefficiency losses which are larger than the gains from appropriated marginal products or a favorable occupational distribution, but particular subgroups (the actual discriminator) may gain. The discriminator suffers a small fraction of the total inefficiency losses of the white community, but he is in a position to appropriate a major fraction of the gain from practicing discrimination. Thus the actual discriminator may gain although the white community as a whole loses. The opposite case

[13] With occupation discrimination, the left side of the expression in note 12 becomes:

$$\left[\sum_{i=1}^{n} \frac{E_i^w}{E^w} MP_{Li} - \sum_{i=1}^{n} \frac{E_i}{E} MP_{Li} \right] E^w$$

where
    E^w = supply of white labor
  MP_{Li} = marginal product of labor in occupation i
    E_i = supply of labor (white plus Negro) in occupation i
    E = supply of labor.

With both wage and occupation discrimination, the above expression is added to the left side of the expression in note 12.

is also possible. An individual discriminator may lose income by refusing to sell his home to Negroes while his neighbors gain. Thus to isolate economic gains or losses for whites as a group does not provide much information about those of specific whites.

HUMAN CAPITAL

Limiting investment in Negro human capital can increase white incomes in several ways. In the short run white consumption possibilities may be expanded, since fewer resources are devoted to education, on-the-job training, and other types of human investment.[14] The return to white human capital also increases when the supplies of Negro human capital are reduced, but part of the gain may be offset by smaller returns to white labor or capital if their distribution depends on the quantity of Negro human capital. The net gains or losses depend on the elasticity of demand for human capital and the exact interdependence between Negro human capital and the productivity of white labor and capital.[15]

In addition to direct gains (or losses) from restricting investment in Negro human capital, restricting capital investment may be one of the best methods of enforcing effective employment, occupation, or wage discrimination. Lack of formal education or on-the-job training may be an effective method to limit the number of Negroes in certain occupations; lack of human investment removes business incentives to cut costs with Negro employees; it confines Negroes to those industries and jobs most subject to cyclical or secular unemployment; it makes wage discrimination more effective

---

[14] The actual effect will depend on the system used to finance human investment. If investment is publicly financed by a proportional or progressive tax system, whites gain when investment expenditures are cut. If a regressive tax system whereby Negroes finance all of their own human investment is in effect, there would be no short-run gains in white consumption.

[15] Analytically, are the gains on the left side of the following expression greater or less than the losses on the right side?

$$(\Delta P)(H^w) \geq < \sum_{i=1}^{n} (\Delta MP_{Li}^w)(E_i^w) + \sum_{i=1}^{n} (\Delta MP_{Ki}^w)(K_i^w)$$

where

ΔP = change in the price of human capital

H^w = quantity of white human capital.

by making Negro labor a complement to white labor rather than a substitute for it; and by denying Negroes managerial experience it may be a means to discriminate against Negro capital (see the following section).

Initially human capital discrimination may arise from a distaste for educating Negro and white children together (though this does not explain lower expenditures on Negro schools), but the result is creation of a monopoly power that can be used to practice other types of economic discrimination. Just as maximizing white gains from employment and occupational discrimination can conflict, human capital discrimination can conflict with occupation and wage discrimination. If wage discrimination were most effective in the skilled occupations (the largest difference between marginal products and wages), maximizing white incomes might call for a heavy investment in Negro human capital.

CAPITAL

This kind of discrimination generally takes one of two forms. Negroes can be prevented from having equal access to the capital markets, or they can be prevented from making efficient use of the capital generated within their own community. By making it difficult for Negroes to use capital, economic discrimination not only prevents them from importing capital, but it also forces the export of their capital. In this case the Negro community exports all production factors and imports consumption goods.

Capital discrimination may be implemented by many techniques. Occupational discrimination and human capital discrimination may deny Negro capital the complementary factor of managerial experience and knowledge; rates of return on capital can be lowered by lack of cooperation from government or legal institutions; discrimination may reduce the real purchasing power of Negro capital; or the threat of white retaliation may make it impossible for Negro-managed capital to enter many areas. Direct price discrimination in the white capital markets may make Negroes pay a premium to borrow or may result in quantitative controls on the amounts or purposes of loans.

White capital loses from discrimination if the rates of return on

capital are higher in the Negro community and white capital re-
fuses to enter. Under Becker's physical distance interpretation of
discrimination there should be little loss of this kind. Whites do
not need to accompany their capital in most cases. However, under
the social distance interpretation the losses may be much greater.
There may be a reluctance to lend money to Negroes since Negro
control over economic resources reduces social distance. The net
gains or losses depend on whether the gains from being able to pay
Negro capital less than its marginal product are greater than the
losses from an inefficient distribution of white capital.[16]

MONOPOLY POWER

This type of discrimination[17] occurs when Negroes are not permitted to enter areas where monopolies result in factor returns
above those prevailing in the competitive areas of the economy.
For instance, if the total number of plumbers is restricted by
union entry terms, their wages may be above competitive levels.
If Negroes are not admitted to the plumbers' union, whites occupy
more than their proportionate share of the fixed number of
plumbing positions and collect all of the monopoly gains without
having to share them with Negroes. This discrimination differs
from occupation discrimination in that the wages in the areas with
monopoly powers are not related to the skills needed. Thus white
losses from the extra training that must be given to less qualified
white are presumably less.[18] The same gains from monopoly privileges can occur in the capital markets.

[16] Analytically, are the gains on the left side of the following expression greater or
less than the losses on the right side?

$$\sum_{i=1}^{n} (MP_{Ki}^{N} - R_{Ki}^{N})K_{i}^{Nw} \gtrless \sum_{i=1}^{n} (\Delta MP_{Ki}^{w})(K_{i}^{w})$$

where
  MP_{Ki}^{N} = marginal product of Negro capital in occupation i
  R_{Ki}^{N} = actual return to Negro capital in occupation i
  K_{i}^{Nw} = supply of Negro capital in occupation i under white control.

[17] R. A. Musgrave first pointed out to me the existence of this variety.

[18] The size of the gains from monopoly power discrimination is given in the
following expression, which indicates the gains from having a more than proportionate share of the monopoly privileges of the economy:

PRICE

Discrimination in selling prices results in gains for the white community if the Negro price elasticity of demand is less than one. In this situation, higher prices produce higher returns for white sellers. If the white community can practice price discrimination in a selective way, discrimination should be applied to those commodities where the elasticity of demand is less than one but not where it is greater than one.

Discrimination in buying prices is similar to wage discrimination (see Becker's theory of discrimination above); the gains depend on the Negro elasticity of supply to the white commodity markets. If supplies are inelastic whites gain, and if they are elastic whites lose. The losses that occur in the process are the inefficiencies that result from a disequilibrium price system.

The housing market is probably the clearest example of price discrimination. By refusing to sell homes in the suburbs to Negroes, whites suffer economic losses, but they also make gains from the higher prices that can then be charged in the central city ghettos. The net gains or losses depend on the relative elasticities of supply and demand inside and outside the ghetto. Since the supply and demand curves for housing are certainly more inelastic in the ghettos, whites as a group gain by housing discrimination, but the whites in the suburbs lose while the slumlords gain. On the other hand, white suburbanites may not perceive this loss if banking institutions refuse to lend money to Negroes (see following section on enforcing discrimination).

$$\left[\sum_{i=1}^{n} \frac{E_i^w}{E^w} (MP_{Li}^M - MP_{Li}^C) - \sum_{i=1}^{n} \frac{E_i}{E} (MP_{Li}^M - MP_{Li}^C) \right] E^w$$

$$+ \left[\sum_{i=1}^{n} \frac{K_i^w}{K^w} (MP_{Ki}^M - MP_{Ki}^C) - \sum_{i=1}^{n} \frac{K_i}{K} (MP_{Ki}^M - MP_{Ki}^C) \right] K^w$$

where

MP_{Li}^M = marginal product of labor in occupation i under conditions of monopoly
MP_{Li}^C = marginal product of labor in occupation i under competitive conditions.

(The capital variables are defined in the same way as those for labor.)

RELATIVE INCOME DISCRIMINATION

Several methods for maximizing absolute white income levels by discrimination have been explored, but the actual white goal may be to maximize relative rather than absolute incomes.[19] Social distance may be maximized in either case. Maximizing absolute incomes is achieved by making any change which will result in higher white incomes, maximizing relative incomes by any change which results in a larger decline in Negro incomes than in those of whites. The conditions for improving relative incomes are even less rigorous than those for improving absolute incomes. For example, wage discrimination can be more vigorously used if it can be carried to the point where the white and Negro losses are equal rather than to the point where white losses first occur.

Enforcement of Discrimination

Both within and between the various types of discrimination there are conflicts among whites. Maximizing the gains for each type of discrimination independently or for any one individual will not result in maximum gains for whites as a group. To maximize the total gains, discrimination must be carried out to the point where the gains from one type are zero or where they are equal to the reductions in gains that it causes to other types, whichever comes first.

Since some whites suffer losses from discrimination—the suburban resident who could sell his home to a Negro for a higher price, the employer who could hire cheaper Negro labor—what mechanism is used to enforce losses on them?

[19] In this case whites will want to maximize the following expression:

$$\frac{\sum_{i=1}^{n} W_i^w E_i^w / \sum_{i=1}^{n} E_i^w}{\sum_{i=1}^{n} W_i^N E_i^N / \sum_{i=1}^{n} E^N}$$

where
W_i^w = white wage in occupation i
W_i^N = Negro wage in occupation i.

When governments play an active role in discrimination, as in South Africa and in many American communities, the powers of government provide the enforcing mechanism.[20] Such powers are the chief means for building and enforcing white monopsony and monopoly powers and preventing countervailing powers from emerging in the Negro community. When a government wishes to practice discrimination, it is the major vehicle for restricting investment in Negro education; it enforces the community desire for discrimination on individual whites who might prefer less of it; it encourages the export of Negro capital by refusing the essential governmental cooperation necessary to run a Negro business; its housing codes prevent whites from selling to Negroes in the wrong locations; and its police powers can be used to discourage Negro retaliation. With central control over the practice of discrimination, compensation can be arranged for whites who lose by it. Thus in South Africa the occupational distribution of Negroes is a subject for negotiation when the wages of white miners are being determined. White wages go up if blacks are allowed into more skilled occupations.

When government does not actively practice discrimination and does not permit explicit legal practices which facilitate it, such as restrictive housing codes or union-management agreements to practice discrimination, enforcement is more difficult. Community or social pressure is one means of forcing whites to accept the concomitant losses. The main mechanism, however, comes from the interlocking nature of the different types of discrimination.

If the various types are viewed separately, there seem to be powerful economic pressures leading to their elimination. Suburban homeowners could gain by selling to Negroes. White employers could increase profits by hiring Negroes. When the several types of discrimination are viewed together, however, the economic pressures are either not present or present in a much more attenuated form.

In the abstract, the white suburban homeowner should be willing to sell to Negroes. Physical distance theories cannot explain his actions. Since he is moving, proximity to Negroes should not

---

[20] In Becker's analysis, government discrimination is treated as merely another discrimination coefficient to be added to the demand curve.

bother him. The social opinions of his ex-neighbors should be irrelevant. Perhaps his utility function includes the opinions of *former* neighbors, and social pressures prevent him from selling to
Negroes. Or perhaps the desire for social distance is the explanation. If Negroes move into neighborhoods where whites formerly
lived and into their old homes, the social distance between blacks
and whites has been reduced. Negroes are only one jump behind.

More likely, other types of discrimination prevent all but a very
few white homeowners from ever having to face this situation.
Other types of economic discrimination result in low Negro incomes. Consequently, Negroes are seldom in an economic position
to bid for the housing of whites. Even if an individual Negro has
sufficient income, he still may be prevented from bidding for a
white home if there is discrimination in lending institutions.
Equal incomes do not lead to the same control over economic resources: a white can buy a more expensive house than a Negro who
has a similar income.

Banks, like individuals, may have very little to lose by discrimination. Since most Negroes have low incomes, the profits from
lending them money are small and may be outweighed by the
losses from white retaliation. If many whites were confronted by
Negro buyers willing and able to pay high prices for housing, or if
banks were faced by the loss of large profits if they did not lend to
Negroes, the strength of residential segregation patterns would be
much less than it actually is.

A similar situation is visible in the lack of job opportunities for
Negroes. Employers should be willing to hire them at lower wages
than are now being paid. Profits would be larger and the employer
need not personally work with them. Social pressures and the individual retaliatory power of white laborers may provide some of the
answers. More likely, employers are seldom confronted by such a
case. In most instances Negroes cannot be hired at lower wages.
Human capital discrimination, in both school and on-the-job training, controls entry into skilled jobs. Thus the employer may seldom see an objectively qualified Negro. Historical practices may
have persuaded Negroes not to apply. The Negroes who do apply
simply lack the skills he needs. Monopoly powers of white labor as
a group may effectively prevent him from paying lower wages to

Negroes or from hiring them. In any case, his losses from not hiring them are obviously minimal, if he seldom or never sees a qualified Negro. Since potential losses are small, less monopoly power is necessary to prevent the employment of the few Negroes who are qualified.

In most cases, plants and firms are willing to hire Negroes for some jobs and not for others: they are not lily-white. Negroes may be hired as sweepers, janitors, and garbage men. There is a social gap between these jobs, which are not within the traditional lines of promotion, and the rest of the jobs in the organization. Negroes are not hired for other jobs since such hiring would reduce social distance between whites and blacks.

Thus it is clear that each type of discrimination makes it easier to enforce other types. Less schooling leads to fewer job skills, easing the problems of occupational, employment, and monopoly power discrimination. Together all of these lead to low incomes, which make price and human capital discrimination easier. Together they reduce Negro political power and make schooling discrimination possible. No matter what type of discrimination is examined, it is reinforced by other types. They exist in a system of mutual support. When all are viewed together, no white perceives great economic losses from discrimination, and consequently there are only minor economic pressures to put an end to it.

Ending Discrimination

Under the Becker theory, there is very little that either governments or Negroes can do to end discrimination.[21] It arises in a free trade environment as a result of the desire of millions of white individuals not to associate with Negroes. Government and Negroes can only attempt to change these attitudes. Antidiscrimination laws merely allow the dispersion of discrimination coefficients to have some effect on the amount of discrimination in society.

---

[21] According to Becker, the government could demonstrate to whites that they suffer economic losses from discrimination, but this is not correct. Becker also states that Negroes cannot gain by retaliation. When terms of trade effects are introduced into his model, this conclusion is also false.

Negroes may find a white who is willing to sell a home to them if he is not prevented from doing so by law. If governments are enforcing discrimination, the median discrimination coefficient governs the amount of discrimination in society, but without government enforcement the marginal discrimination coefficient governs the amount.

Under the theory of discrimination presented in this chapter, there are many actions which governments and Negroes can take to end discrimination. Many of the effects of discrimination rest on monopoly or monopsony powers of whites. Governments and Negroes can attempt to break down these powers in government, labor, and business institutions.

White Gains

Since economic theory does not provide definitive conclusions about the white gains or losses from discrimination, empirical evidence must be examined. Even if it can be demonstrated that whites can gain from discrimination, this does not prove that they do. They may simply be inefficient practitioners of discrimination.

Data from the United States census of population for 1960 are used as the source of the estimates presented;[22] but data limitations mean that the formulae developed earlier cannot be applied directly. Rough approximations must be made to the desired equations, but these can be illustrative even if not definitive.

White *employment* would have fallen if white and nonwhite employment rates had been equalized in 1960. To evaluate the gain from a favorable employment picture, the extra white employment must be multiplied by some income figure. Assuming that white employment was enlarged by squeezing the nonwhite community out of its average job, the white employment gain should be multiplied by the average nonwhite income. By this calculation, whites gained $0.8 billion in 1960 by having a lower un-

---

[22] U.S. Bureau of the Census, *U.S. Census of Population: 1960*, Vol. 1, *Characteristics of the Population*, Pt. 1, *United States Summary* (1964), and *Occupation by Earnings and Education*, Final Report PC(2)-7B (1963).

employment rate than nonwhites.[23] If whites replaced nonwhites with above-average jobs, the white gain would be even larger.

However, if nonwhites are paid less than their marginal products due to wage discrimination, and if white incomes represent actual marginal products, the white employment gain should be multiplied by average white incomes, yielding a gain to white labor of $1.6 billion. But this is not a net gain to the entire white community. Higher wages for white labor reduce the income to white capital, which loses $0.8 billion because of fewer opportunities for practicing wage discrimination. Thus on the basis of both assumptions, there is a net gain of $0.8 billion to the white community.

White gains from *wage discrimination* can be calculated on the assumption that wage differences within sex, educational, and occupational categories are due to wage discrimination rather than to real differences in productivity. Generally, the more detailed the categories the more accurate the assumption, but more detailed categories may not make it possible to eliminate all the real differences in productivity if the classifications themselves are inaccurate. If seven years of Negro education is not equivalent to seven years of white education, the two groups should not be classified together. Unfortunately, there is little that can be done about this problem. The estimates presented here are based on two sexes, twelve occupations, and six educational categories—or one hundred forty-four individual cells. If white incomes in each of these cells reflect real marginal products, the gain to the white community from wage discrimination is merely the summation of the difference in white and Negro earnings in each category multiplied

[23] This was calculated according to the following formula:

$$[(U \times LF^w) - (U^w \times LF^w)]I^N$$

where

U = national unemployment rate
LF^w = white labor force
U^w = white unemployment rate
I^N = nonwhite income for employed workers.

Unemployment rates are from U.S. Bureau of Labor Statistics, *Employment and Earnings and Monthly Report on the Labor Force* (February 1966), pp. 20, 21. Labor force and income statistics are from U.S. Bureau of the Census, *U.S. Census of Population: 1960*, Vol. 1, *Characteristics of the Population*, Pt. 1, *United States Summary* (1964), pp. 488, 580.

by the number of Negroes in the cell. On these assumptions, wage discrimination raised white incomes by $4.6 billion in 1960.[24]

If whites received the benefits of wage discrimination, white incomes would not represent real marginal products, because of the additional income from discrimination. The observed differential between white and nonwhite incomes would be twice as large as the real productivity differential. Thus the net gain would be $2.3 billion rather than $4.6 billion; however, to the extent that the benefits from wage discrimination were kept as retained earnings by white capital, the gains would be greater than $2.3 billion.

White gains from *human capital discrimination* can be calculated on the assumption that whites are distributed across the educational spectrum in the same manner as the population as a whole rather than according to their more favorable actual distribution. With sixteen educational categories and with white income in each cell assumed to represent marginal productivity, a favorable distribution resulted in a white gain of $7.9 billion in 1960.[25]

The gains from *occupational discrimination* cannot be calculated by simply distributing whites across occupations in the same manner as the population as a whole, since the occupational distribution partially reflects the educational distribution. To calculate

[24] The formula used was:

$$\sum_{j=1}^{2} \sum_{i=1}^{12} \sum_{k=1}^{6} [(I_{ijk}^{w} - I_{ijk}^{N})E_{ijk}^{N}]$$

where

I_{ijk}^{w} = white income in sex j, occupation i, and educational category k
I_{ijk}^{N} = nonwhite income in sex j, occupation i, and educational category k
E_{ijk}^{N} = nonwhite employment in sex j, occupation i, and educational category k.

Since the full breakdown of earnings by sex, occupation, and education is available only for males aged eighteen to sixty-four, while the breakdown for sex and occupation is available for males and females of all ages, data for males eighteen to sixty-four were used to calculate a percentage correction factor that was applied to data for all males and females.

[25] This was calculated by the following formula:

$$\left[\sum_{j=1}^{2} \sum_{k=1}^{8} \frac{P_{jk}^{w}}{P^{w}} I_{jk}^{w} - \sum_{j=1}^{2} \sum_{k=1}^{8} \frac{P_{jk}}{P} I_{jk}^{w} \right] P^{w}$$

where

P_{ijk}^{w} = white persons in educational category k and of sex j
P^{w} = white persons in experienced labor force
I_{jk}^{w} = white income in educational category k and of sex j
P_{jk} = total persons in educational category k and of sex j
P = total persons.

the gains from occupational discrimination without allowing for this interaction would be to double-count some of the gains from educational discrimination. A favorable white distribution across sex, occupational, and educational categories (144 cells) yields a gross gain of $12.4 billion,[26] but the educational gains of $7.9 billion must be subtracted in order to calculate the effects of occupational discrimination alone. Actually, this net gain of $4.5 billion also includes gains from monopoly power discrimination in the labor market, since the white income level in each cell may partially result from monopoly powers.

The total gain from employment, wage, human capital, occupational, and labor monopoly discrimination was $15.5 billion, or $248 per member of the white labor force in 1960 (the corresponding nonwhite loss was $2,100 per member of the labor force), but what about the white labor losses? Losses occur principally if the supply of nonwhite labor to the white community is reduced. With both an income and a substitution effect from discrimination, it is impossible to specify the results a priori. The nonwhite community has two methods for reducing its supplies of labor. Nonwhites can withdraw from the labor force or they can work for themselves or other nonwhites. Since nonwhite labor participation rates are higher than those for whites (56.3 versus 55.2 percent), they probably have not withdrawn from the labor force in the aggregate, though this total figure is composed of lower participation rates for men (72.1 versus 78.0 percent) and higher rates for women (41.8 versus 33.6 percent).[27] Since the null hypothesis is unknown, it is impossible to say that the nonwhite labor force is not affected by discrimination, but the probable effects are not large. Similarly, very few nonwhites have been able to use their

---

[26] Here the formula was:

$$\left[\sum_{j=1}^{2} \sum_{i=1}^{12} \sum_{k=1}^{6} \frac{P_{ijk}^{w}}{P^{w}} I_{ijk}^{w} - \sum_{j=1}^{2} \sum_{i=1}^{12} \sum_{k=1}^{6} \frac{P_{ijk}}{P} I_{ijk}^{w} \right] P^{w}$$

where

P_{ijk}^{w} = white persons in occupational category i, educational category k, and sex j

P^{w} = white persons in experienced labor force

I_{ijk}^{w} = white income in occupation i, educational category k, and sex j

P_{ijk} = total persons in occupation i, educational category k, and sex j

P = total persons.

[27] U.S. Bureau of the Census, *U.S. Census of Population: 1960*, Vol. 1, *Characteristics of the Population*, Pt. 1, *United States Summary* (1964), pp. 213–14.

labor within the nonwhite community rather than sell it to the white community, judging by the number of nonwhites who are self-employed farmers (2.2 percent for nonwhites and 4.0 percent for whites), the number of nonwhites who are self-employed managers (1.4 percent for nonwhites versus 3.9 percent of whites), and the small number and size of nonwhite corporations. Although there is little evidence that the supply of Negro labor to the white community has been reduced quantitatively, qualitative factors must be considered. These may have caused a larger reduction in nonwhite labor than would appear from the raw data. With under-investment in Negro human capital, the supply of Negro labor measured in efficiency units (units adjusted for quality) is certainly less. Working to offset the inefficiency losses from less Negro labor are the white gains from capital discrimination, monopoly power discrimination against nonwhite capital, and price discrimination. White economic gains from these three sources have not been considered.

Probably an estimate of $15 billion plus or minus $5 billion would be a good range for the annual white gains (or Negro losses) from discrimination in the United States. The $15 billion, however, is not an estimate of the maximum gain that would be achieved by discrimination. Considering the inefficiencies with which the system is actually run, an efficient system would probably yield a much larger gain.

Since discrimination produces large economic gains, there are important vested interests in its continuation. Programs to eliminate discrimination must take these interests into account; economic self-interest cannot be counted on to aid in eliminating discrimination. The magnitude of the gains also indicates that elimination would have a powerful impact on the distribution of income for nonwhites.

Impact on Potential Output

Whites (individually or collectively) may or may not be able to gain from discrimination, but the total potential output of the country is always less, since productive resources are inefficiently allocated. Although some of the reduction is caused by using members of the preferred group in jobs where their individual productivities are below those of members of the disadvantaged groups, the main reduction in potential output is probably caused by discrimination in education and underutilization of the nonwhite labor force.

To the extent that there is a surplus of labor of all types and skills, eliminating discrimination and reshuffling the labor force would result in a redistribution of income but in no real gains in actual output. To keep general gains from a higher utilization of white capacity distinct from the gains from eliminating discrimination, aggregate economic policies are assumed to be specific enough to provide markets for the extra output gained by ending inefficiencies but not to have any impact on white utilization levels.

The production function approach outlined in Chapter 3 provides a convenient method for estimating the impact of discrimination on potential output. Four effects can be isolated. (1) Eliminating discrimination would reduce nonwhite unemployment and thus raise the stock of labor used in production. (2) The improvements in capacity utilization resulting from the increase in nonwhite employment would cause a small increase in productivity levels. (3) Raising nonwhite educational levels to those of whites would increase the amount of human capital contained in the labor force, with a consequent increase in output. (4) Equipping the larger labor force (measured in efficiency units) with the average amount of capital would cause a further increase in output. Neither increasing human capital nor providing physical capital is costless. Real resources must be devoted to raising educational levels and increasing investment. To determine net gains, these costs must be deducted from the increases in potential output.

Equalizing white-nonwhite unemployment rates in 1966 would have raised nonwhite employment by 356,000, by decreasing nonwhite unemployment from 7.5 percent to 3.4 percent (see Table 7-1). In addition to excessive unemployment, nonwhites suffered from underemployment relative to whites; they worked only 37.6 hours per week while whites worked 40.7 hours.[28] The elimination of this difference as well as the unemployment difference would have increased total labor supplies by 1.5 percent.

[28] U.S. Bureau of Labor Statistics, *Employment and Earnings* (January 1967), p. 103.

TABLE 7-1

Labor Supply, by Color, United States, 1966

(*In thousands*)

Item[a]	White	Nonwhite	Total
Labor force	68,424	8,617	77,041
Employment	66,096	7,968	74,064
Unemployment	2,328	649	2,977
Unemployment rate (percentage)	3.40	7.53	3.86

Source: *Manpower Report of the President, April 1968*, pp. 224, 230–231.
a. Data are for persons fourteen years of age and over in the civilian labor force.

Before the output effects of this increase can be estimated, adjustments must be made for the different amounts of human capital embodied in white and nonwhite workers. Assuming that the quality of labor is proportional to the number of years of schooling completed, the human capital of a nonwhite worker represents 85 percent of that of a white worker, since the figure for his median years of schooling completed is 10.5 compared with 12.3 years for whites.[29] If total employment in 1966 were adjusted to a "white equivalent" basis, 72.9 million people were employed. Adjusting the raw increase in nonwhite labor supplies to the same basis yields an increase in the white equivalent labor force of 1.1 percent. Using the elasticity of output with respect to labor (λ) from the production function (Appendix A), output would rise by 0.9 percent. Improvements in utilization resulting from the lower unemployment level would raise output by another 0.1 percent. If the larger labor stock were equipped according to the 1966 average capital-labor ratio, output would rise by 0.2 percent, using the production function elasticity of output with respect to capital. But investment would have to increase by \$7.3 billion to accomplish this goal.

Programs to equalize white and nonwhite education levels in the labor force would increase the white equivalent labor force by another 1.6 percent. As a result, output would expand by 1.3 percent, and maintaining the effective capital-labor ratio would cause

[29] *Manpower Report of the President, April 1968*, p. 259.

a further increase of 0.3 percent. The cost of the additional plant and equipment would be $10.2 billion and there would also be costs in increasing education levels of nonwhites. To equalize education levels would require 15 million man-years of education. At the average 1964 costs of $559 per man-year of education in public elementary and secondary schools,[30] educational expenditures would have to rise by $8.4 billion.

If all of the outlined changes were made, private output would rise by 2.83 percent or $18.8 billion per year, at the cost of an investment of $25.9 billion. Although additional costs would be incurred over time to cover the depreciation of both human and capital equipment, the annual increase in output of $18.8 billion compares very favorably with an initial investment of $25.9 billion. Assuming a twenty-year rate of depreciation on the extra human and physical capital, the investment produces a net return of 65 percent per year.

Since most of those in the labor force with a low level of education are above the normal school-leaving age, the costs of a man-year of schooling might be much higher than the national average for younger people. On the other hand, concentrating on on-the-job training, where productivity effects are probably larger than those for general education, might reduce the calculated costs. Additional benefits would also accrue from the elimination of the constraints on the efficient use of existing men and machines. Although there are enough unknowns to challenge any specific dollar estimate, rough calculations would certainly indicate that eliminating discrimination is a profitable social investment even when regarded strictly from an economic point of view.

Implications

Even if the preceding calculations are not precise, the social benefits from eliminating discrimination far outweigh any possible economic losses. The purpose of studying discrimination is not to show that the white community can make economic gains from

[30] U.S. Bureau of the Census, *Statistical Abstract of the United States: 1967* (1967), p. 120.

eliminating it. Some whites will certainly lose, and whites as a group may also lose. The purpose of this chapter has been to examine the methods by which discrimination is put into effect. Such knowledge makes it possible to design programs that might be used to eliminate discrimination.

Eliminating government discrimination has the highest priority since it is the most effective weapon to create and enforce many of the monopoly powers that are behind the different types of discrimination. Additionally, government powers are used to suppress the conflicts of interest among whites that might otherwise emerge. Human capital discrimination probably is the next most important type to eliminate; it holds a key role because it can be used as an informal method for enforcing many of the other types. Attacking human capital discrimination will not raise Negro incomes by itself, since wage, employment, and occupational discrimination would also have to be eliminated, but eliminating human capital discrimination would make the enforcement of these other types difficult in the absence of government discrimination.

CHAPTER VIII

Limitations and Alternatives

Raising workers' productivity and eliminating market imperfections, with resulting wage raises for workers, are necessary measures in the contest against poverty and discrimination, but they are by no means sufficient in themselves. They cannot benefit a large number of individuals. For some people there may be no known method to raise their productivity to acceptable levels. For others the program costs may be prohibitive. In these cases other programs must be designed.

Families and individuals who are now outside the labor force represent the largest group who cannot be aided by the productivity approach. There may be no one in the family who can take advantage of education, training, or better job opportunities. For these families programs to enhance personal productivity are worthless. There are other persons who, because of handicaps of age, lack of education, lack of training, poor work habits, or a deprived prior existence cannot be brought up to acceptable levels of productivity. They can no longer be trained or educated. The errors made in the past are irreversible.

There are two ways of providing income for those who cannot earn an acceptable one. The first is guaranteed jobs and sheltered employment—useful work requiring little skill, paid out of public funds, adapted to the competence of the workman. The second is simply direct income transfers—payments made without work performed in return. They will be discussed in later sections of this chapter.

Families outside the Labor Force

Families with no wage earner made up only 8 percent of the total number of families in 1967, but they accounted for 41 percent of the families with incomes of less than $3,000, 45 percent of those with less than $2,000, and 43 percent of those with less than $1,000.[1] There are many reasons why people may be outside the labor force: (1) They are unable to work because of physical handicaps or illnesses. (2) Their individual productivity is below the level tolerated by industry and government.[2] They have learned that no employer will hire them and hence have left the labor market. (3) They have left the labor force since there are plenty of preferred workers to fill any job vacancy at existing utilization levels; they do not believe that they can find work, and they are right. (4) Institutional constraints, such as age limits, may keep them out of the labor market. (5) The net returns from working (wages minus the costs of working) simply may not be large enough to cover the nonmonetary benefits from not working. This may be explained by laziness, but it may also be because a mother needs to remain at home with her children.

Labor statistics indicate that a large percentage of poor families are outside the labor force, but even these statistics understate the importance of the problem. As general productivity levels rise, those who are able to take advantage of better job opportunities or of government programs to increase individual productivity are gradually drawn out of the poverty pool. Those who cannot benefit are left at the bottom of the income distribution and consequently represent an increasing fraction of the poor.

The trend can be seen in the changes from 1947 to 1966. Families with no wage earners in the labor force rose from 16 percent to 38 percent of the total number of families with incomes of less

[1] U.S. Bureau of the Census, *Current Population Reports*, Series P-60, No. 59, "Income in 1967 of Families in the United States" (1969), p. 41.

[2] Technically, some firm should be willing to hire such workers at a low wage, but labor markets are not completely flexible on this matter. Legal minimum wages or minimums enforced by unions or community pressures may prevent wages from falling. In addition, workers may withdraw from the labor force rather than accept pay far below the social norm.

than $3,000 (in 1963 dollars). While the total number of families in that range was declining from 11.7 million to 7.6 million, the number of poor families with no wage earner was increasing from 1.9 million to 2.9 million. Poverty among those families actually declined from 82 percent to 71 percent over the same period, but the percentage decline was not large enough to offset their growing number. As productivity levels rise and government productivity programs succeed, the trend will continue. The bottom of the income distribution will be increasingly made up of those not in the labor force.

The percentage of families with no wage earners is only slightly higher for Negroes than for whites (10 percent versus 8 percent). Such families accounted for 26 percent of all Negro families with incomes under $3,000 in 1966—a smaller percentage than that for whites (42 percent), since a much larger fraction of the Negroes who are actively working earn low incomes. As productivity levels rise and job opportunities for Negroes expand, Negro families with no wage earner will compose an increasing fraction of the total number of poor families. As a result, productivity programs are of greater relative importance to the Negro community than to the white community, but the same absolute proportion of the Negro population will need other programs if they are to have acceptable incomes.

Improving utilization rates in the economy would shift the demand curve for labor upward, raise the marginal productivity of labor, provide more jobs, and attract some new workers into the labor force. The basic problem would remain, however. Most of the families now outside the labor force would remain outside at any conceivable utilization rate. Increasing the utilization rates attracts new workers into the labor force, but few of them come from families which are now completely outside. Such families would be reduced by less than 3 percent for every 1 percentage point decline in unemployment.[3] They are relatively insensitive to economic opportunities, since 70 percent of the total number of families with no wage earners are headed by a female or by the aged. The incidence of poverty within each of these groups declined in the postwar period, but the decline was more than matched by a rising

[3] See App. E.

number of families in the group. Between 1947 and 1965, the proportion of families with incomes below $3,000 (in 1963 dollars) which were headed by a female rose from 16 percent to 26 percent, and the proportion headed by the aged from 21 to 37 percent. Under the official definition of poverty,[4] the same concentration emerges: in 1965 households with female heads accounted for 26 percent of the poor and those with aged heads, another 37 percent. Among Negro households, female heads accounted for 33 percent of the total number of poor and the aged for 19 percent. Thus, while families with aged heads are less significant among Negroes than among whites, families with female heads are more significant.

If the poor families with aged heads, with female heads, and with no wage earner in the labor force are combined, they account for 67 percent of the total number of families with incomes below $3,000 in 1965. Under the official definition of poverty the composition changes slightly, but the same three groups account for 69 percent of the poor households and among Negroes for 59 percent of the total number of poor households.

Families Poor Although in the Labor Force

Although families outside the labor force compose a sizable fraction of the poor, a still larger portion—60 percent—of the families headed by females or the aged are in the labor force but poor nonetheless. Some workers are unable to work enough hours to earn acceptable incomes. The same factors which lead to nonparticipation for some lead to limited participation for others. Others are able to work full time, but are simply unable to earn adequate incomes.

Society may also increase the size of the poverty problem for females and the aged by giving them a genuine economic option not to be in the labor force. Mandatory retirement rules, earned income restrictions under Social Security, 100 percent tax rates on public assistance payments, and many other factors indicate that

[4] See pp. 4, 22.

society prefers to let the elderly rest and provide "at-home" mothers. Many households headed by aged and females now have members in the labor force to augment income and thus avoid living in poverty. Society might choose to give these individuals freedom to avoid poverty without joining the labor force. If so, perhaps the labor force participation rates among the elderly and female family heads should be much lower than they actually are. In that event income redistribution measures for families outside the labor force might need to be more extensive than the poverty statistics would indicate.

In any case, society must begin to make some consistent decisions about who should and should not be in the labor force. These are essentially social rather than economic decisions. If society wishes to eliminate poverty among the elderly by putting them to work, society must be consistent enough to eliminate mandatory retirement rules, earned-income limits under Social Security, and the many other factors that encourage or force the elderly out of the labor force. The same is true for mothers with young children. If society wants female family heads to work, it must eliminate the existing high tax on their incomes under the public assistance laws. If society does not want these two groups to work, it ought not to force them into it by giving them inadequate incomes. Poverty programs for the two groups must not be based on the supposition that they ought to work.

Workers beyond the Aid of Productivity Programs

Families that are or should be outside the labor force are much easier to identify than are individuals whose personal handicaps cannot be overcome by productivity programs. Given private and public rules on mandatory retirement ages, individuals who are poor and nearing retirement probably compose the only group that productivity programs cannot aid. Perhaps they can be trained for good jobs, but the length of time they would be able to hold the jobs makes the benefits of training small. In 1967, 15 percent of the families with incomes of less than $3,000 were headed by individuals between the ages of fifty-five and sixty-four.[5] Productivity programs for these persons would be of limited value because they will soon leave the labor force. Many individuals with low incomes may also be untrainable or trainable only at prohibitive costs. The psychological, physical, educational, and cultural deprivations of the past may be irreversible.[6]

Society may have no method of rehabilitating many individuals, but the individuals cannot be identified in advance of attempts at rehabilitation. Therefore rehabilitation programs must be closely coordinated with guaranteed jobs or direct income transfers and must be widely available to determine which persons require such jobs or income transfers. Furthermore, the eligibility requirements for jobs or income transfers must be flexible enough to include people from a wide variety of groups.

Guaranteed Jobs

For those who are outside the labor force because they are unacceptable to private employers or those whose personal handicaps cannot be overcome by productivity programs, sheltered employment provides one possible answer. Work is provided for the individual by the public rather than the private sector. Wages are set on the basis of the desired income distribution rather than the productivity of the worker. Thus the job is partially a work creation program and partially an income transfer program. In many cases it may be easier and cheaper to create jobs which are tailored to the capabilities of the worker rather than develop his skills to fit available jobs. Subsidies can be given to private employers to hire specific workers, or the government can become an employer of last resort for those whose productivity levels are not high enough to be attractive to private industry or public agencies.

Because of the difficulties of subsidizing private industry and competing with employed workers, the "Automation Commission"

[5] U.S. Bureau of the Census, "Income in 1967 of Families in the United States," pp. 32–33.

[6] Alvin Poussaint, "The Psychology of a Minority Group with Implications for Social Action," paper delivered at RAND Workshop on Urban Affairs, Santa Monica, Calif., January 1968.

has suggested that the guaranteed jobs be created in public services or private nonprofit institutions.[7] As it points out, finding useful jobs with low skill requirements is not difficult in public services. Millions of jobs can be found in schools, hospitals, conservation, natural beautification, and city sanitation. Wages would probably exceed a worker's productivity in these jobs, but needed services would be produced.[8] Thus the real cost is much lower than that of a straight income transfer.

Perhaps the major benefit of guaranteed jobs is not lower real costs but the resultant self-respect of the worker. Self-support may not be economically necessary or desirable, but many individuals want to earn their own incomes. The personal dignity created for them by purposeful work may be a compelling reason for guaranteed jobs. In a society which places a high premium on self-reliance, society should be extremely careful to provide work for everyone who wants it. If an individual has accepted society's values concerning the desirability of work, he should be accommodated. Direct income transfers are involved, but they are hidden from both society and the individual.

There are three major objections to guaranteed jobs: (1) Employed workers may feel threatened by subsidized workers. (2) Guaranteed jobs may create a class of dead-end jobs that are unacceptable to the poor and stigmatized by the rich. (3) Public institutions require a stable labor force to be efficient; the rapid turnover and mobility involved would lead to inefficiency.

The first objection can be met pro forma by requiring that the jobs be used to expand public services and not to cut labor costs for government or nonprofit institutions, but it can never be avoided in reality. There is no method of knowing how many people would have been hired if the guaranteed jobs had not existed.

Opposition on the second score might be reduced if guaranteed jobs are coordinated with efforts to increase workers' productivity by creating associated training programs for those who wish to use

[7] National Commission on Technology, Automation, and Economic Progress, *Technology and the American Economy*, Vol. 1 (Government Printing Office, 1966), pp. 35–37.

[8] If the current lack of public services in these areas is caused by market imperfections which systematically lead to underconsumption in the public sector, wages may not be less than a worker's marginal product.

them. Programs such as the Neighborhood Youth Corps use guaranteed jobs to attract individuals into training programs, to provide some training, and to serve as an income transfer mechanism. This feature should be retained in any national system of guaranteed jobs.

In circumstances where many do not wish to accept employment in what are known as dead-end jobs, and since most of the suggested public service jobs are actually such jobs, training opportunities are particularly important. Jobs may be accepted only if they can lead to something better. Since those who cannot move into better jobs because their handicaps are insurmountable are not known a priori, the door should always remain open for individuals to advance. Many of them may not use the training opportunities, but the existence of the opportunities is important to the success of guaranteed job programs in order to prevent the jobs from looking like second-class leaf-raking jobs both for those who may advance and for those who cannot.

The third objection cannot be avoided in any way. Society must simply decide if the benefits of guaranteed job programs exceed the costs of inefficiency that they may cause in public institutions.

If a system of guaranteed jobs were established without a system of direct income transfers, a large number of workers might shift to the jobs. If wages were set at a minimum wage of $1.75 per hour, either most of the workers who are now making less than $3,640 per year would shift to guaranteed jobs or their employers would raise wages to this level.[9] The opportunity to qualify for guaranteed jobs should be open to all, however, to help maintain the social prestige of the jobs. In 1966, 40 million workers made less than $3,640 per year, but many of these were the elderly, the young, and women who did not want full-time employment and did not come from poverty families.[10] A rough calculation indicates that there are potentially 15 million eligible workers who might want a guaranteed job. Since many would be retained by their

[9] There would be some inflationary pressures as a result.

[10] U.S. Bureau of the Census, Current Population Reports, Series P-60, No. 53, "Income in 1966 of Families and Persons in the United States" (1967), p. 46. Guaranteed jobs would presumably be open only to secondary workers from poor families, but they might also be used to solve teen-age unemployment if it is deemed important.

present employers, it is difficult to estimate how many would change jobs.[11] In addition to employed workers, some additional workers from poor families might be attracted into the labor force, but this would probably be a much smaller number.

Direct Income Transfers

To eliminate and not merely reduce poverty, some system of direct income transfers must be used. Income would be redistributed to create the desired distribution, and in the process some individuals would be given incomes without working for them. No system of guaranteed jobs and productivity programs will be able to raise every household above the poverty line. Many households are outside the labor force and the members cannot work under any circumstance. In addition, society may not wish to force all individuals to work.

If direct income transfers could be limited to those who cannot work and those whom society wishes to free from the economic necessity of having to work, they would present few economic problems. Income would simply be transferred to these households. The problems are generated by spillover effects on other individuals. Those whom society wants in productivity or guaranteed job programs may be encouraged not to enter these programs; those whom society wants in the labor force may be encouraged to drop out. Individuals now working may stop; others may refrain from starting to work. To determine how many people would not work because of the existence of income transfers requires knowledge of individual preferences between work and leisure, but it also depends on the rate at which leisure can be transformed into income.

An income transfer plus a one-for-one reduction in the size of the transfer for every dollar earned (a 100 percent tax rate) certainly provides no financial incentive to work, but the size of the actual decrease in work effort is unknown.[12] If the tax rate is less

[11] The supply of labor in some occupations, such as domestic servants, would probably be severely reduced.

[12] An experiment to investigate this problem has been undertaken in New Jersey by the Office of Economic Opportunity.

than 100 percent, economic theory cannot predict the direction of the work effort, much less its empirical magnitude. Presumably lump-sum income transfers plus high marginal tax rates reduce work effort. If the marginal utility of income rises over some income ranges, however, work effort may actually rise in the face of high marginal tax rates and positive income transfers. Empirical evidence on the importance of monetary incentives is very spotty and their impact on low-income families is almost unknown.[13]

Suggestions such as the negative income tax are designed to reduce the adverse incentive effects that may result from programs like public assistance, which for many years was taxed at a rate of 100 percent.[14] If tax rates are lowered, work incentives are enlarged. Less leisure must be sacrificed to earn a given income. However, another problem is created. A marginal tax rate of less than 100 percent means that some individuals who are above the poverty line must receive aid if no one is to be left below the poverty line. In order to provide aid for the poor, much of the aid must go to those who are not poor. The problem is less important if we remember that poverty is preferably defined as a band, not as a state existing below a specific line, and that poverty definitions might be based on relative rather than absolute incomes. The income transfers are still going to those with low incomes. The problem can be serious, nevertheless, if budget constraints are severe and society wishes to give its limited aid to those at the bottom of the income distribution. The more the aid is concentrated at the bottom, the greater the adverse incentive effects.

To design direct income transfer programs, society must make compromises on two fronts. First, it must decide how much it is going to let the optimal distribution of work incentives influence the optimal distribution of purchasing power. Second, it must decide how it is going to balance the incentive effects of lower marginal tax rates against the need to concentrate aid on the poor.

Although there is no way around these two dilemmas, there are ways to minimize them. Efforts can be made to find techniques of

---

[13] For a summary of existing evidence, see Christopher Green, *Negative Taxes and the Poverty Problem* (Brookings Institution, 1967), Chap. 8.

[14] The 1967 amendments to the Social Security Act reduced the tax rate to less than 100 percent. Small amounts of income can be earned.

income distribution which minimize the spillover effects on work incentives. If a variable could be found that was perfectly correlated with income and could not be altered by the individual, this variable could be used as a criterion for receiving direct income transfers. Since aid would not be given on the basis of income and since the criterion variable could not be altered, no incentive effects could occur.

No one variable or system of variables eliminates the work incentive and spillover problems, but there are variables that move in the right direction. Age is probably the best example. Poverty is extensive among the aged, and age cannot be altered. If eligibility for a direct income transfer system is limited to the aged, both the work incentive effects and the spillover effects are limited to the aged. The result is a reduction in the severity of the clashes between the distribution of purchasing power and work incentives and between marginal tax rates and giving aid to those who do not need it. This is especially true if society does not want the elderly to work. In this case adverse work incentives are desired, and there is no clash between the distribution of incentives and purchasing power. No aid need be given to those above the poverty line, since a 100 percent tax rate can be used without an undesired effect on incentives.

However, using female household heads as a criterion variable for public assistance provides a good example of the problems that are endemic to efforts to reduce incentive effects by finding surrogate variables for income. Limiting aid to households with female heads meets only one of the two tests for a good criterion variable. Poverty is highly correlated with female household heads, but female-headed families can be independently created by male desertion. Using these households as a criterion variable cuts adverse work incentives and limits aid to those who need it most, but it does create an incentive to desertion. The number of desertions caused by the desire to obtain public assistance is unknown and may be small, but any public policy which encourages desertion is unfortunate.

Children's allowances constitute another program that attempts to find a criterion variable. Decisions to have children can obviously be altered by the individual, but the incentive effect of children's allowances on these decisions is also unknown.[15] As in the case of families with female heads, however, any impact is probably unfortunate. There is a more fundamental objection to children's allowances, however. Children are not highly correlated with low incomes. Basing aid on children might solve many incentive problems, but most of the aid would be given to children in families that do not need aid under any income criteria.[16]

Since good criterion variables are difficult or impossible to find, income transfer programs will always be difficult to organize if budget constraints are severe or adverse incentive effects are important. There is no perfect method for limiting aid to the poor without creating adverse work incentives.

If budget constraints are not severe and adverse work incentives are not important, negative income tax proposals[17] provide the best system of income transfers. Allowances would be set to raise all households to the poverty line. If the allowances were greater than the household's income, the household would have a negative taxable income. A person with such an income, instead of sending a tax payment to the government as he would with a positive taxable income, would receive a check from the government to raise his income to the size of his deductions. The tax system currently covers only positive incomes and excess allowances are ignored. Negative income tax proposals have the overwhelming advantage of being an impersonal system of income transfer which does not destroy individual dignity. Social Security payments provide the best analogy; they are in part a disguised income transfer which is acceptable to both society and the individual since they have the facade of being acquired by right. Negative income tax payments appear in the same light, and this constitutes their primary advantage over transfer systems such as public assistance.

A negative income tax program with a marginal tax rate of 50 percent would cost $25 billion to bring every household up to the poverty line. Approximately $12 billion would go to those

---

[15] Many countries, such as Canada, have children's allowances but do not have higher birth rates as a result.

[16] James Tobin, "Do We Want Children's Allowances?" *New Republic*, Nov. 25, 1967, pp. 16–18.

[17] Green, *Negative Taxes*.

who are technically below the poverty line and the rest would go to individuals above that line.[18] If the positive incentive effects on those who are now on welfare were larger than the negative incentive effects on those who are now working, the costs would be less. If the reverse were true, the costs would be higher.

If budget constraints are severe, society may wish to limit aid more narrowly than negative income tax proposals would allow without very high marginal tax rates. One method of doing this is to lower the marginal tax rate on public assistance payments. Negative income tax proposals would have the advantage of disguising the transfer of income, but marginal tax rates can be lowered on any income transfer system. If the marginal tax rate on public assistance payments is lowered, those on public assistance can be encouraged to work without affecting those who are not eligible for public assistance. Creating effective incentives in the public assistance system is difficult to accomplish. State and local governments must cooperate. Different localities have very different welfare laws and welfare payments.

Integrating poverty programs can provide a good method of reducing adverse work incentives. Direct income transfer systems should be combined with complementary productivity and guaranteed job programs. The smallest work incentives are offered when income transfers are universally available and work is not available. The greatest work incentives occur when work is universally available and income transfers are not available. If an income supplement is to be universally available, as it must be to eliminate poverty, maintaining work incentives almost demands that work be universally available. Providing good job opportunities with training and advancement possibilities is a very necessary condition for maintaining work incentives.

Implications

Any analysis of poverty indicates that poverty cannot be eliminated without direct income transfers. Many people simply cannot

[18] *Ibid.*, p. 141, Plan D-1: Adjusted, and p. 23.

enter the productive economy, others can be brought in only at prohibitive costs, and society may wish to encourage still others to stay out. Some system of a guaranteed annual income is essential.

Quantitatively, direct income transfers have approximately the same effects on both white and Negro incomes. Without the transfers poverty can be eliminated in neither community. Guaranteed jobs, however, would have a much greater relative effect on the Negro incomes. Most white workers earn incomes above the levels proposed under guaranteed jobs; most Negro workers do not. Eliminating the lower end of both the white and Negro income distributions would substantially close the gap between them.

CHAPTER IX

A Review of the Findings

This chapter provides a brief summary of the conclusions reached in this book. In Chapter 1 the reader was urged to consider the evidence critically and to examine the analysis with skepticism. In the same vein, the recapitulation in the following pages is not offered as revealed doctrine. It is intended merely to jog the memory of the reader for his own further analysis and reflection upon the problems of poverty and discrimination.

Income

According to the official definition of poverty, the proportion of the population living in poverty has slowly but steadily declined in the period since the Second World War, at a rate that would require some four decades to eliminate it. If the easier poverty cases are removed first, an increasing proportion of hard-core cases will slow the rate and more than four decades will be necessary. However, if long-run relative income distribution definitions of poverty are used, such as 50 percent of median incomes, there has been no decline in the postwar period. The distribution of income in this period has not changed.

Nor has discrimination declined. The average Negro family income has consistently remained near 55 percent of the white income. For a given average income level the white and black distributions have similar shapes, but the Negro distribution lags

153

approximately thirty years behind the white. On the basis of relative measures such as these, discrimination has neither declined nor increased. In absolute terms, however, between 1947 and 1967 the average income gap between white and Negro families widened from $2,300 to $3,100 (in 1967 dollars). Relative measures indicate a stable pattern of discrimination, absolute measures a more intense pattern.

Whatever definitions are used, past and projected changes in the income distributions indicate the need for special programs if poverty and discrimination are to be eliminated. General economic growth and foreseeable changes in the structure of the private economy will not eliminate either of them. Programs must be specifically designed to alter the distributions of income.

Poverty

Poverty can be eliminated without understanding its causes simply by transferring income to the poor. If this is not to be the sole instrument, however, and if society wants individuals to earn their incomes by producing goods and services, the structural causes of poverty must be identified. Programs to combat the factors that produce poverty cannot be designed without both qualitative and quantitative knowledge of the factors. The relative size of their impact is important in determining the priorities and magnitudes of different programs.

An econometric model was developed to isolate and quantify the causes of poverty and to explain variations in its incidence among states. The distributions of human capital, physical capital, and employment opportunities were shown to have important effects on both white and Negro poverty. Quantitatively their effects seem similar, but the factor of racial discrimination affects only Negro poverty and not white. Everything else being equal, poverty is greater for Negroes. Thus white and Negro poverty are not identical. The income redistribution goals of the war on poverty may be color blind, but policy instruments must be color conscious. The package of programs that will cure white poverty will not cure Negro poverty. Something extra is needed.

Discrimination further complicates the analysis of poverty, since it is not just another independent factor which can be added to the analysis. It may have some independent effects, but primarily it works through the other causes of poverty. If incomes are assumed to be a simple function of education levels, there are still three effects of discrimination on Negro incomes. Preventing Negroes from acquiring education reduces income—more of them are poor because they have less education. Negroes have lower marginal returns to education—the twelfth year of education may raise white incomes by $500 and those of blacks by only $250. The absolute incomes associated with varying educational levels differ—improving the level from two and one-half to six years of schooling increases white incomes from $1,900 to $3,200 and eliminates white poverty, but increases black incomes only from $1,600 to $2,400, leaving them still poor. As a result, education may be an efficient variable to raise white income levels, but inefficient where Negro income is concerned.

Thus programs which would eliminate all white poverty would only partially eliminate Negro poverty. Specific programs must be designed to eliminate discrimination, oriented to Negro poverty, not white.

Economic Policies

Increasing the utilization of economic resources would reduce both poverty and discrimination. Reducing unemployment by 1 percentage point would reduce the number of persons in poverty by 1.25 million; the long-run effects of higher resource utilization would be even greater. Unbalanced labor markets and severe shortages of labor would create strong incentives for making the changes necessary to reduce poverty and discrimination. Alterations in training programs, employment standards, and individual incentives would further reduce poverty and the inequities in the distribution of income. Improvements would be especially noticeable for the Negro. Tight labor markets would increase both white and Negro incomes, but the favorable effects would be larger for Negroes. Lowering the unemployment rate from 7 percent to 3 percent would increase Negro family incomes from 50 percent of white incomes to 60 percent.

Although unbalanced labor markets have sizable direct effects on incomes and important indirect effects on other sources of higher incomes, such as training programs, higher utilization rates cannot totally eliminate either poverty or discrimination. Other changes are needed, but these may require tight labor markets as necessary conditions. Analysis indicates that 3 percent unemployment should be a major target for the war on poverty and discrimination.

Human Capital

Individual skills and knowledge—human capital—are an important determinant of the distribution of income. For the poor and for Negroes, rational factors lead to systematic underinvestment in their own human capital. The result is a widening gap in the human capital between the rich and the poor, between whites and blacks.

By means of the human capital function income flows were examined and the returns to education and experience were isolated for whites and Negroes in the North and South. The marginal returns to education and experience are much lower for Negroes than for whites. Negroes, and especially those in the South, receive fewer benefits from job experience. Lower wages for the same work, less on-the-job training, and a lack of adequate physical capital with which to work offer a partial explanation.

More important than the marginal returns to either education or training are the complementarities among education, training, physical capital, and technical progress. The complementarities between education and training are so great that programs to increase them must be carefully coordinated if either type of program is to have the expected payoff in terms of increasing incomes. The complementarities vary among races, regions, and occupations, but the joint effects of having both education and training are four times as large as the sum of their separate effects.

No program to raise incomes through raising education will succeed unless other measures are also taken. Raising functional literacy standards to eighth or tenth grade standards may be an important ingredient in raising incomes, but the effects will not be apparent unless it is combined with training opportunities and job opportunities. Eliminating discrimination is necessary if Negro education is to have a significant effect. As long as there is discrimination, more education produces little payoff.

Job experience or on-the-job learning is a major source of the gap between Negro and white incomes. Thus a major proportion of the task of increasing Negro human capital must be achieved in the private sector of the economy. Governments can provide significant incentives for private actions, but government education programs will have small returns unless the private job market can be cracked at the same time.

Physical Capital and Technical Progress

The distribution of income is much wider than would be predicted from the distribution of human capital alone. Only a small part of the difference can be explained by the distribution of the ownership of physical wealth; much must be explained by imperfect labor markets. With imperfect labor mobility, individuals who work with little physical capital or in areas with little technical efficiency receive low incomes, while those in areas with high capital-labor ratios and high technical efficiency earn large incomes. Competitive pressures do not equalize incomes for individuals with the same human capital. To explain the difference between the actual distribution and the income distribution that would be predicted on the basis of human capital, market imperfections must be severe and the distributions of physical capital and technical progress quite uneven. The impact of market imperfections is particularly harsh on Negroes.

A major part of the effort to eliminate low incomes among both whites and Negroes must be directed toward narrowing the distributions of physical capital and technical progress or toward making them irrelevant. Improving the mobility of the labor force is of major importance. This can be achieved directly by better labor market information or by providing incentives for mobility, indirectly by encouraging industrial firms to move into Negro areas.

Discrimination

Under Becker's theory, government actions can have little effect on discrimination, which occurs because whites are willing to pay in order to avoid associating with Negroes. To effect a change, attitudes must be altered or whites must be bribed to mingle with blacks. Unless the government is willing to pay whites more than their discrimination premium, they will not cooperate.

Although this theory may explain some white actions, an alternative theory suggests that much discrimination is based on the monopoly powers of whites. Without such powers racial prejudices would have less impact on Negro incomes. With monopoly powers, however, whites may gain financially and enforce discriminatory practices that substantially lower Negro incomes. Functionally, monopoly can be reduced without changing the attitudes of the whites who discriminate. Equality need not wait until man has goodwill toward all races or until the government is willing to bribe him to be nice to his neighbor.

Quantitatively, the monopoly powers of the white community vis-à-vis the black community are a major force leading to lower Negro incomes and higher individual white incomes. Negro losses and white gains from discrimination amount to approximately $15 billion per year. In addition, discrimination causes a large reduction in the potential level of output of the American economy. Negro economic resources are not fully utilized and white resources are inefficiently utilized as a result of discrimination. Efficiency losses amount to approximately $19 billion per year.

The institutions of government are an important link in implementing discrimination. Either directly through legal restrictions or indirectly through harassment and expenditure decisions, the coercive powers of the white community flow through local, state, and federal government institutions. Eliminating discrimination in all levels of government may be one of the most effective means of eliminating the effects of discrimination throughout the economy.

Persons outside the Labor Force

Programs to raise the earnings of individual workers cannot aid many families which are either completely or partially outside the labor force. Guaranteed jobs or sheltered employment have been suggested as a solution, but many cannot benefit from employment of any kind. For them, direct income transfers are necessary. In the long run, the negative income tax appears to be the most promising solution.

Examination of the problems and opportunities presented by both guaranteed jobs and direct income transfers reveals the need for integrating productivity programs, guaranteed job programs, and direct income transfers. All are necessary, each can function more efficiently if the other programs are also present, and each can be damaged if the others are not well coordinated with it.

Strategies for Eliminating Poverty

Coordinated programs for creating tight labor markets, improving the distribution of human capital, increasing labor mobility, ending discrimination, and providing for those outside the labor force are all necessary to eliminate poverty and discrimination. No one program can work by itself. Theoretically direct income transfers are an exception to this rule, but politically they seem to be unacceptable.

As the analysis has shown, reducing the income gap between rich and poor and closing the income gap between black and white are interrelated problems. To succeed in either project would automatically bring improvement in the other; but no set of programs, except direct income transfers, can achieve either of them without recognizing the interaction between poverty and discrimination. Programs to eliminate poverty will not work for Negroes unless they operate on racial discrimination. Programs to put an end to racial inequality will not work unless they act on the causes of poverty which afflict black and white alike.

APPENDIXES

APPENDIX A

The Marginal Productivity of Labor

The aggregate production function used to study the marginal productivity of labor in Chapter 3 is a modified Cobb-Douglas function containing terms for the quantity of capital and labor, level of capacity utilization, economies of scale, embodied technical progress in capital and labor, and disembodied technical progress, as seen in equation (A-1). The particular form of the function was first suggested by Solow and later modified by the author.[1] Other production functions could be used, but comparing the differences among them is a study in itself.[2]

$$(A-1) \qquad Y(t) = e^{a + bU^2} e^{\alpha t} \big[K_x(t)^{1-\lambda} L_z(t)^{\lambda} \big]^{\gamma}$$

where

Y = output
t = time
U = unemployment rate
K_x = capital stock measured in efficiency units

$$K_x = \left[\sum_{v=-\infty}^{t} (1 + x)^v B(t - v) I(v) \right] \big[1 - U \big]$$

[1] Robert M. Solow, "Technical Change and the Aggregate Production Function," *Review of Economics and Statistics,* Vol. 39 (August 1957), pp. 312–20; "Investment and Technical Progress," in Kenneth J. Arrow, Samuel Karlin, and Patrick Suppes (eds.), *Mathematical Methods in the Social Sciences, 1959* (Stanford University Press, 1960); "Technical Progress, Capital Formation, and Economic Growth," *American Economic Review,* Vol. 52 (May 1962), pp. 76–92; Lester C. Thurow and L. D. Taylor, "The Interaction Between the Actual and the Potential Rates of Growth," *Review of Economics and Statistics,* Vol. 48 (November 1966), pp. 351–60. See this paper for a more detailed discussion of the choice of the production function.

[2] Lester C. Thurow, "Disequilibrium under Alternative Production Functions," to appear in a volume honoring Thomas Balogh, edited by Paul Streeten and published by George Weidenfeld.

$I(v)$ = investment in year v

$B(t-v)$ = amount of capital investment from year v surviving in year t

x = rate of embodiment in capital

L_z = labor man-hours measured in efficiency units

$L_z = L(1 + z)^t$

L = observed man-hours

z = rate of embodiment in labor

α = rate of growth of disembodied technical progress

γ = economies of scale

λ = elasticity of output with respect to labor.

The unknown parameters of the production function are found by using exogenous information and by regression techniques. External information on the rate of growth of education and productivity, plus experimentation with different rates of embodiment in capital and labor, indicated that a production function with a 1 percent per year rate of embodiment in labor and a 4 percent per year rate of embodiment in investment provided the best results. Neither economies nor diseconomies of scale were found to exist, but adjustments for changes in utilization were necessary. The capacity utilization variable is non-linear. A shift in unemployment from 5 percent to 4 percent raises output by 0.24 percent; a shift from 4 percent to 3 percent raises output by 0.19 percent. Disembodied technical progress is estimated at 1.17 percent per year and the elasticity of output with respect to labor is 0.83 (see regression (A-2),[3] which gives the results in the estimating form for the period 1929–65).[4]

$$(A\text{-}2) \quad \ln \frac{GNP_p}{K_{04}} t = \frac{0.6048 - 0.0269U_t^2 + 0.01167t + 0.8304 \ln \frac{L_{01}}{K_{04}}}{(0.0159) \quad (0.0030) \qquad (0.00122) \qquad (0.0262)}$$

$$\bar{R}^2 = 0.99 \qquad \text{d.w.} = 1.35 \qquad \text{d.f.} = 0.33 \qquad S_e = 0.022$$

[3] Thurow and Taylor, "The Interaction Between the Actual and the Potential Rates of Growth." The coefficients are slightly different, since new capital stock estimates have been published in the interim and the production function has been estimated with two-stage least squares.

[4] Private gross national product is from *Survey of Current Business*, various issues; unemployment data are from U.S. Bureau of Labor Statistics, *Employment and Earnings and Monthly Report on the Labor Force*, various issues; capital stock is from *Survey of Current Business*, Vol. 47 (February 1967), p. 20 (gross stocks, constant cost 2 series); labor stock is from *Economic Report of the President, January 1967*, p. 249. The equation was estimated with two-stage least squares to obtain estimates of the structural coefficients. The model in which it is estimated is in "A Policy Planning Model of the American Economy," available from the author.

where

GNP_p = private gross national product in constant 1958 dollars

L_{01} = labor man-hours with embodied technical progress of 1 percent per year

K_{04} = capital stock with embodied technical progress of 4 percent per year in investment (constant 1958 dollars).

The marginal product of labor is found by differentiating the production function with respect to labor:

(A-3)
$$\frac{\partial Y(t)}{\partial L(t)} = e^{a+bU^2}e^{\alpha t}K_{x_1}(t)^{[(1-\lambda)(\gamma)]}[(1+x_2)^t]^{\gamma\lambda}\gamma\lambda L(t)^{\gamma\lambda-1}.$$

Here the marginal product of labor depends upon five factors; improvements in them raise the marginal productivity of labor: (1) *Human capital* (education and training). Efficiency man-hours grow faster than observed man-hours, producing growth in the marginal product per observed man-hour. The impact of this factor is represented by $[(1+x_2)^t]^{\lambda\gamma}$. (2) *Physical capital.* The innovations embedded in new plant and equipment (technical progress embodied in capital) further magnify the effects of a rising capital stock. These innovations lead to an even larger increase in the capital-labor ratio when capital is measured in efficiency units rather than observed units. The impact is represented by $K_{x_1}(t)^{[(1-\lambda)(\gamma)]}$. (3) *Disembodied technical progress* (improvements in the organization of the economy and the more efficient use of men and machines). The impact is represented by $e^{\alpha t}$. (4) *Utilization levels.* Since overhead capital and labor cannot be altered in proportion to changes in output, improvements in utilization rates raise the marginal productivity of labor and deteriorations lower it. When the rates improve, some of the labor and capital necessary to increase output is already employed. The capital and labor stocks do not have to rise in proportion with the increase in output: they are merely used more efficiently. The impact of utilization rates is represented by e^{a+bU^2}. (5) *Labor stock.* The marginal product of labor depends on the amount of labor already employed. The greater the current employment, the less the marginal productivity of labor. As the employment of labor increases, the amount of capital per worker falls. The result is falling output per worker. The impact of the labor stock is represented by $\gamma\lambda L(t)^{\lambda\gamma-1}$. Disembodied technical progress and utilization rates shift the production function, while the other factors represent movements along it.

Empirical estimates of the marginal productivity of labor are generated by inserting the parameters and data of the production function into equation (A-3), the marginal productivity of labor. According to these results a decline in unemployment from 4 to 3 percent raises the marginal productivity of labor by 0.2 percent. Disembodied technical progress and technical progress embodied in labor cause annual increases in labor's marginal product of 1.17 percent and 0.83 percent respectively. The elasticities of the marginal productivity of labor with respect to capital (measured in efficiency units) and labor (measured in observed units) are identical in magnitude (0.17), but the signs differ. The stock of capital is positively related to the marginal product of labor, while the stock of labor is negatively related.

The marginal product of labor for 2,000 hours of work per year in the private American economy rose from $2,678 in 1929 to $7,236 in 1965 (in constant 1958 dollars). Growth of the marginal productivity of labor accelerated between 1929 and 1965. In the period before 1947, the average rate of growth of the marginal product of labor was 2.4 percent. Since 1947 the average has been 3.2 percent. The acceleration was caused by a faster rate of growth of the capital stock. In the earlier period capital stocks actually fell in observed units and rose only slightly in efficiency units. In the postwar period capital stocks have risen more rapidly. The result is faster growth of the marginal productivity of labor.

The marginal product of labor contrasts with an actual rise in the compensation of employees from $2,293 to $5,660 for 2,000 hours of work. A large gap seems to exist between earned income and calculated marginal products. Reasons for the extensive gap are investigated elsewhere,[5] but the gap does not seem to be a product of the particular choice of the production function used in regression (A-2).[6] A wide variety of production functions produce similar gaps between the marginal product of labor and the compensation of employees. Possible explanations of the gap include the existence of actual economies of scale, the classification of returns to managerial innovations, systematic differences in avoidance of risk by capital and labor, monopoly powers, market imperfections, disequilibrium conditions, the nonhomogeneity of labor, and differences between gross returns and private returns caused by taxes.

Other studies of the sources of growth have used observed income shares to study changes in the marginal productivity of capital and

[5] Lester C. Thurow, "Disequilibrium and the Marginal Productivity of Capital and Labor," *Review of Economics and Statistics*, Vol. 50 (February 1968), pp. 23–31.

[6] Thurow, "Disequilibrium under Alternative Production Functions."

labor. As long as all factors of production are paid their marginal products, indirect studies of the sources of growth through observed changes in income shares and the explicit marginal productivity approach should yield the same sources of growth. Marginal products and incomes do not seem to be in equilibrium, but it is still interesting to compare the sources of growth found by the two techniques.

Existing studies of growth have concentrated on explaining the growth of output and not the growth of labor's marginal product. There are no theoretical problems in translating a study of output growth into a study of the growth of labor's marginal product, but practical data problems make it easier to translate the production function approach into a study of the sources of output growth rather than the reverse. Then a direct comparison can be made between the sources of growth found using regression (A-2) and Denison's classic study of growth.[7]

According to Denison, the growth of the labor stock (adjusted for quality) accounted for 54 percent of the growth of output between 1929 and 1957, the growth of the capital stock accounted for 15 percent, and disembodied types of technical progress accounted for the remaining 32 percent (see Appendix Table A-1). The corresponding figures from regression (A-2) are: labor, 33 percent; capital, 26 percent; and disembodied technical progress, 41 percent.

A large part of the observed differences result from differences in the data being analyzed. Denison analyzes the growth of the net national product. Regression (A-2) analyzes the growth of the gross product of the private economy. If regression (A-2) is adjusted by adding the public sector of the economy and by subtracting capital consumption allowances, the two sets of estimates are similar. According to the adjusted results from the regression, labor accounts for 44 percent of output growth, capital 17 percent, and disembodied technical progress 39 percent.

Based on a comparison of the sources of growth from Denison and from regression (A-2), the sources of growth of the marginal productivity of labor presented in Chapter 3 would seem to be roughly compatible with Denison's results. During a period when the public sector has grown very rapidly, the sources of growth of the private sector of the economy can be very different from the sources of growth of the total economy. In the period between 1929 and 1957, capital is much more

[7] Edward F. Denison, *The Sources of Economic Growth in the United States and the Alternatives Before Us* (Committee for Economic Development, 1962).

TABLE A-I

Percentage Contribution of Selected Sources of Output Growth
in the United States between 1929 and 1957

	Percentage contribution		
Sources of growth	Denison	Regression (A-2)	Adjusted regression (A-2)[a]
Growth of the labor stock	54	33	44
Quantity	20	11	n.a.
Quality	34	22	n.a.
Growth of the capital stock	15	26	17
Quantity	n.a.	5	n.a.
Quality	n.a.	22	n.a.
Disembodied technical progress	32	41	39
Economies of scale	11	0	n.a.
Increase in knowledge	20	n.a.	n.a.
Market efficiency	1	n.a.	n.a.
Total	100	100	100

Sources: First column, Edward F. Denison, *The Sources of Economic Growth in the United States and the Alternatives Before Us* (Committee for Economic Development, 1962), p. 266, sixth column; second and third columns, author's estimates. Figures are rounded and will not necessarily add to totals.

n.a. Not available.

[a] The public sector of the economy is added to, and capital consumption allowances are subtracted from, regression (A-2) to put the two studies on an equivalent net national product basis.

important and labor is much less important in the private economy than they are in the total economy. Future projections of the sources of growth will depend heavily on the expected division of growth between the public and private sectors of the economy.

APPENDIX B

A Critique of the Poverty Model

Poverty is a vicious circle. A lack of education may cause poverty, but poverty may lead to a lack of education.

(1) In reality causation moves in both directions. No analytical model can unravel such a system and turn it into a system of unidirectional causation. Real causation simply does not work in one direction. Many chemical reactions work in the same manner, working in both directions, but one direction dominating. The dominant direction of reaction, it is hoped, is the one specified in the poverty model developed in Chapter 3. Since causation does not run simply from the independent to the dependent variables in the model, perhaps the chapter should have been called the correlates rather than the causes of poverty. The chapter title depends on one's belief about the strength of the reactions in each direction. Does causation run primarily from low education to poverty or from poverty to low education, from being outside the labor force to poverty or from poverty to being outside the labor force?

(2) A poverty model is searching for the factors that cause the incidence of poverty to change over time. Consequently, the model should be estimated with time series data. Unfortunately only the most limited and elementary hypotheses can be tested with time series data on the incidence of poverty. The statistical variation in the incidence is not sufficient to test the hypotheses outlined in the poverty model. To test realistic hypotheses cross-sectional data must be used. Yet such data may not be an adequate representation of how the world changes over time. The differences between cross-sectional and time series consumption functions are vivid illustrations of the problem.

Some information on the adequacy of cross-sectional poverty models can be gained by making time series projections.[1] The poverty model

[1] See pp. 43–44.

underestimates the decline in the incidence of poverty from 1960 to 1965, since it does not take into account increases in productivity within industries. Variation within industry productivity is not important in cross-sectional analysis, but it is important in time series analysis. There may be other factors of the same nature.

(3) The poverty equation should be estimated with alternative definitions of poverty to see how the definition of poverty affects the coefficients of the model. The logical choice would be to rerun the model using the Social Security Administration definitions of poverty. Unfortunately, the official definition of poverty is not available on a state-by-state basis. Shifting to the official definition of poverty would principally affect the coefficient for the percentage of families headed by a farmer. This coefficient would be smaller, since the official poverty line for farmers is $1,925, not $3,000.[2]

(4) The proper degree of disaggregation is always a subject of controversy. Since poverty is a family phenomenon, perhaps the family is the proper unit of observation. Aggregation uses up degrees of freedom and may hide the true variability of results. Yet if data are too disaggregate, random noise may begin to dominate the results. States were chosen as the unit of observation since data are readily available, there is enough variability in the incidence of poverty to test alternative hypotheses, and there are enough observations to preserve a reasonable number of degrees of freedom. Metropolitan areas would provide an alternative set of observations, but relevant data are much more difficult to acquire.

(5) Different variables in the poverty equation may interact with each other. An explicit test was carried out for interactions between education and race.[3] The interactions did not prove to be significant. Similarly, the poverty equation performed well at predicting both white and nonwhite incidences of poverty. If there were significant interactions between being nonwhite and the other variables in the equation, a good nonwhite projection should not have occurred. This evidence does not mean interactions can be ignored. In Chapter 5 they proved to be very significant. Given the level of aggregation and the range of incomes studied in the poverty model, interactions did not seem important. At different income levels and with more detailed investigations, they may be very important.

[2] See Chap. 3, note 9.
[3] See pp. 38–39.

APPENDIX C

Median Incomes and the Analysis of Poverty

It was indicated in Chapter 3 that median incomes, although they have customarily been of great value in analyzing poverty, fail to supply data on the sources of income growth.

If the factors that lead to rising incomes have equal proportionate effects on all workers,[1] the sources of income growth for those with low productivities can be found by analyzing the sources of income growth for labor in general. By definition the same factors have the same effects on workers at all levels of productivity. Most of the existing econometric analysis of poverty is more a test of the hypothesis that different growth factors have equal proportionate effects on all individuals than it is an investigation of the causes of poverty. The incidence of poverty is explained by median family incomes (a proxy for the average of productivity) and unemployment.[2]

Using the official definition of poverty, over 90 percent of the postwar variance in the incidence of poverty can be explained by changes in median incomes alone. The same close relationship is seen in cross-sectional data. Over 90 percent of the variance in the state-by-state incidence of poverty can be explained by the median family income in the state. In both time series and cross-sectional analysis, poverty and median incomes are closely associated. To say that median incomes and poverty move together says nothing about the causes of movement for either of them.

To say there are high correlations between median incomes and the

[1] Except for a random disturbance term.

[2] Gallaway has shown that changes in poverty are strongly related to changes in median family incomes over time. In his simplest formulation, a $100 increase in real median family incomes reduces poverty by about 0.5 percentage point. Lowell E. Gallaway, "The Foundations of the 'War on Poverty,'" *American Economic Review*, Vol. 55 (March 1965), p. 127.

incidence of poverty is merely another way of saying that the dispersion of income has not changed. As long as the dispersion of income is constant, there will always be a high correlation between median incomes and the percentage of population below some line. If indices of dispersion are constant, or if there is a high correlation between poverty and median incomes, the sources of growth are having similar effects on all segments of the income distribution.

In one sense the variables actually used in the poverty model are a set of proxy variables for median incomes, since they represent factors which determine median incomes as well as poverty incomes. Although the poverty model is designed to explain the incidence of poverty, the same set of variables can be used to explain median incomes. Only the coefficients differ. The poverty model is designed to determine some of the causal factors influencing both poverty and median incomes.

Statistically to explain poverty as officially defined by median incomes is to introduce a near tautology. Median incomes can logically grow without lowering the incidence of poverty, but this is not likely to happen. If the incomes of families located between the median income line and the poverty line were growing, and if the incomes of families below the poverty line were not growing, median incomes could grow without affecting poverty. Income growth of families located above the median income line does not affect the median and thus cannot produce the same effect. Thus in the normal case median incomes and the official definition of poverty are partially measuring the same phenomenon. Under alternative definitions of poverty the near tautology does not exist. If poverty is defined as 50 percent of the median income, a rising median income does not automatically lead to less poverty.

Although the poverty model partially escapes from the problems of relating poverty and median incomes, the escape is not complete by any means. What the model does avoid is having to use the observed differences in state wage levels within a particular industry. This is significant since wage scales in most industries have a range of 2 to 1 from the highest wage state to the lowest wage state.[3] The model reduces the problems presented by median incomes, but it does not eliminate them.

[3] U.S. Bureau of Labor Statistics, *Employment and Earnings Statistics for States and Areas, 1939–63* (1964).

APPENDIX D

Principal Component Analysis

The seven variables in the poverty regression in Chapter 3 explain the variation in the incidence of poverty by state, but they do not indicate that there are seven independent factors. Several of these variables are closely related to each other and are probably slightly different manifestations of more general explanatory variables. As might be expected, the percentage of families with no one in the labor force is closely related to the industrial structure of the state. The percentage of Negro family heads and heads with less than an eighth-grade education also move together.

High correlations between explanatory variables do not affect the qualitative importance of different causal variables. Two explanatory variables can be closely related to each other and both still be important causes of poverty. The problem which arises is one of statistics rather than causation. Explanatory variables may be so highly correlated with one another that it becomes difficult, if not impossible, to disentangle their separate influences and to obtain a reasonably precise estimate of their relative effects. By using principal component analysis, however, it is possible to evaluate more clearly the independent dimensions which might be present among the various explanatory factors used in the poverty model. A new variable is constructed (the first principal component) which is a linear combination of the explanatory variables. It explains the maximum amount of variation of the explanatory variables, subject to the restriction that it is independent of every other principal component. The same procedure is followed in calculating the second principal component after the influence of the first principal component has been removed, and so on.

Among the seven variables in the poverty regression, the first four principal components account for 98 percent of the total variation of all seven variables (see Appendix Table D-1, where the percentage of

TABLE D-I

Percentage of Trace of Seven Principal Components of the
Independent Variables in the Poverty Equation

Principal component	Percentage of trace
First	54.68
Second	28.29
Third	13.39
Fourth	2.26
Fifth	0.89
Sixth	0.50
Seventh	*

Source: Author's estimates, based on poverty equation (see text and Chap. 3).
* Less than 0.005.

the trace gives the percentage of the total variation explained by each component), and only the first three are really important. The first component accounts for 55 percent of the total variation, the second for 28 percent, and the third for 13 percent. Basically, there would appear to be only three independent dimensions among the seven variables which appear in the poverty model. The seven variables could be reduced to three without sacrificing much information.

An obvious further step is to see whether it is possible to identify the first four principal components. This objective can be accomplished only by correlating the original explanatory variables with their principal components, thereby isolating which variables move with which principal components. These correlations are given in Appendix Table D-2.

The first principal component can be identified with a general measure of the quality of the potential labor force, as shown by the negative correlations with the percentage of families headed by a Negro, the percentage of families with no one in the labor force, and the percentage of families with low education levels. All three of these groups suffer from handicaps in competing for jobs and in taking advantage of economic progress.

Both the second and third principal components are positively related to the percentage of families headed by farmers and negatively related to the industrial structure of a region. Since farming is part of the industrial structure of a region (the quality of the industrial structure goes up as the percentage of farmers goes down), both of these principal components can be identified with different aspects of the quality of the industrial structure of a region.

TABLE D-2

Simple Correlation between the Independent Variables and Their
First Four Principal Components in the Poverty Equation

Variable	Principal component			
	First	Second	Third	Fourth
Families living on farms	0.09	0.71	0.69	−0.03
Families headed by a nonwhite	−0.95	−0.27	0.14	0.01
Families with no one in the labor force	−0.54	−0.05	0.08	0.71
Family heads with 0–7 years of school completed	−0.65	0.70	−0.30	−0.06
Population age 14 and above who worked 50–52 weeks per year	−0.04	−0.70	0.38	−0.51
Index of industrial structure	0.04	−0.60	−0.73	−0.11
Dummy for Alaska and Hawaii	−0.54	−0.51	0.28	0.22

Source: Author's estimates, based on poverty equation (see text and Chap. 3).

The second principal component is also positively correlated with the percentage of families with low education levels and negatively correlated with the percentage of the population who work full time. These correlations are consistent with the previous identification of the second principal component as the quality of the industrial structure. Education is related to the industrial structure in the long run, since educational demands depend on the type of industries which are located in the region, but education is also related because high wage industries do not locate in regions with low education levels. Over time, good employment opportunities, which provide a large number of full-time jobs, also increase labor force participation rates by attracting workers into the labor force. Thus, the correlation with education levels and full-time workers fits into the identification of the second principal component as a measure of the industrial structure. This identification is confirmed by ranking the states according to the coefficients of the second principal component. States with a poor industrial structure are at the bottom of the list and those with a good structure are at the top.[1]

[1] Ignoring the special cases of Hawaii, Alaska, and the District of Columbia, the top ten states are Utah, California, Washington, Delaware, Massachusetts, Connecticut, New Jersey, New York, Nevada, and Colorado, and the bottom ten states are South Dakota, Alabama, West Virginia, South Carolina, North Dakota, Tennessee,

While the third principal component also represents the industrial structure, a ranking of states by the coefficients of this principal component reveals that it is primarily distinguishing between farm and non-farm states. Both southern and northern nonfarm states have high rankings, while the low rankings go to the midwestern and plains farm states.[2]

The fourth principal component is related to the percentage of families with no one in the labor force, and negatively related to the percentage of the population who worked full time. These correlations would seem to identify this component as a general measure of the labor force participation rates in an area.

Principal component analysis can also be used to see whether any of the other variables considered for inclusion in the poverty equation add an independent dimension to the study of the causes of poverty. Principal components were computed with six additional variables,[3] but the first four principal components still explained 98 percent of the total variation of all thirteen possible variables, and the correlations found between these thirteen variables and the first four principal components confirmed the original identification of the principal components.

In sum, the incidence of poverty seemingly can be explained by four general dimensions: (1) the quality of the human labor force as viewed through discriminatory eyes; (2) the quality of the industrial structure; (3) the amount of farming; and (4) a measure of labor force participation rates.

Arkansas, Mississippi, North Carolina, and Kentucky (proceeding from top to bottom). The indexes of the industrial structure are high for the first group and low for the second group.

[2] The top ten states are West Virginia, Rhode Island, Pennsylvania, Massachusetts, Louisiana, New Jersey, Connecticut, New Hampshire, New York, and Maine, and the bottom ten states are Wyoming, Montana, Kansas, Oklahoma, Mississippi, Idaho, Iowa, Nebraska, North Dakota, and South Dakota (proceeding from top to bottom). Farm population is low in the first group of states and high in the second.

[3] The other six variables considered were: (1) the percentage of families headed by a female; (2) the percentage of families with heads over age sixty-four; (3) median school years completed; (4) percentage of families where head has less than eighth-grade education, minus those with college education; (5) state unemployment rates; and (6) an occupational index.

APPENDIX E

The Impact of Aggregate Demand on Three Explanatory Variables in the Poverty Model

This appendix presents detailed calculations for the estimates presented in Chapter 4 of the reduction in poverty connected with the following explanatory variables: percentage of population fourteen years old and above who worked 50–52 weeks per year; percentage of families that were living on farms; and percentage of families that had no one in the labor force.

Full-Time Work

To determine the relationships between unemployment (the general measure of human resource utilization) and the percentage of the population working on full-time jobs, observed movements in the percentage of full-time workers must be corrected for changes in the age-sex composition of the labor force, as seen in equation (E-1). When the teen-age population rises, the proportion of full-time workers in the population falls. Labor force participation rates are lower for teenagers; also they traditionally do not hold full-time jobs. When female participation rates rise, however, the proportion of full-time workers in the population rises. Although the percentage of the female labor force with full-time jobs is below the corresponding percentage of the male labor force, some of the new female workers do hold full-time jobs. This leads as a consequence to a smaller fraction of the labor force working on full-time jobs, but a larger fraction of the population holding full-time jobs.

In a 1950–63 time series each of the variables has the expected effects:

(E-1) $W_h = 33.7617 - 0.5996U + 0.2951P_f - 0.5129T_e$

           (3.5836) (0.1159)   (0.1525)   (0.2122)
              **   **   *

$\overline{R}^2 = 0.82$ d.f. $= 10$ d.w. $= 1.62$ $S_e = 0.39$

where

W_h = percentage of population aged fourteen and above who worked
  50–52 weeks per year and 34 or more hours per week
U = unemployment rate
P_f = participation rate for females
T_e = proportion of the population aged fourteen and above who are
  teen-agers.

Note: The standard errors of the coefficients are shown in parentheses.
* Coefficient significant at 0.05 level.
** Coefficient significant at 0.01 level.

When unemployment declines and female participation rates rise, the
percentage of full-time workers increases. When the teen-age population rises, the percentage of full-time workers falls. A decline in unemployment of 1 percent leads to a 0.75 percentage point increase in
full-time workers.[1]

Farmers

From 1947 to 1965 the percentage of farm families fell from 12.8 percent to 6.1 percent of total families.[2] Farm mobility can be explained
by relative income opportunities in farming and by the availability of
alternative nonagricultural employment opportunities (see equation
E-2). Reductions in farm incomes relative to nonfarm incomes and increases in nonagricultural job opportunities encourage farmers to move

[1] Part of the increase in full-time workers is caused by induced increases in female
participation rates. A one percent fall in unemployment leads to an induced increase
in female participation rates of 0.5 percentage point. This accounts for 0.15 percentage point of the 0.75 percentage point increase in full-time employment. Alfred
Tella, "The Relation of Labor Force to Employment," Industrial and Labor Relations Review, Vol. 17 (April 1964), pp. 454–69.

[2] These percentages have been corrected for changes in the definition of "farmer."
Before correction, the number of farmers drops from 17.5 percent to 6.1 percent. U.S.
Bureau of the Census, Trends in the Income of Families and Persons in the United
States: 1947 to 1960, Technical Paper No. 8 (1963), p. 44, and Current Population
Reports, Series P-60, No. 51, "Income in 1965 of Families and Persons in the United
States" (1967), p. 18. For a more complete discussion of farm mobility, see Brian
Bartney Perkins, "Labor Mobility between Farm and Nonfarm Sector" (Ph.D. thesis,
Michigan State University, 1964).

into urban areas. Since the elasticity of farm mobility with respect to relative incomes is 0.2 (evaluated at the means) while the elasticity with respect to nonagricultural job opportunities is 2.2, the impact of employment opportunities clearly dominates relative income effects.[3] Since farm incomes are less than 60 percent of nonfarm incomes,[4] the small response to marginal changes in relative farm incomes is not surprising. Nonfarm incomes are still substantially higher than farm incomes.

The differences in the size of the elasticities with respect to relative income and urban employment opportunities are fortunate from a policy standpoint. If both elasticities were large, there might be major problems in simultaneously operating programs designed to cure farm poverty by raising farm incomes and programs designed to cure farm poverty by encouraging mobility into urban areas. Since the income elasticity is small, both types of policies can be pursued without much conflict. Higher farm incomes would keep some families on the farm, but not very many.

From 1947 to 1963 the following results occur:[5]

(E-2) $\quad F = 228.4661 + 0.0420I_r - 25.6083 \ln J + 4.7276D_1 + 2.6835D_2$

$$(18.1589) \quad (0.0229) \quad (2.0565) \quad (0.4894) \quad (0.2979)$$
$$** \qquad\qquad ** \qquad\qquad ** \qquad\qquad **$$

$$\overline{R}^2 = 0.99 \qquad \text{d.w.} = 2.44 \qquad \text{d.f.} = 12 \qquad S_e = 0.31$$

where

F = percentage of families headed by farmers

I_r = median farm family income as a ratio of median nonfarm family income

J = civilian nonagricultural employment

D_1 and D_2 = dummies to account for changes in the definition of farmers in 1949 and 1959.

Note: The standard errors of the coefficients are shown in parentheses.
** Coefficient significant at 0.01 level.

[3] The large intercept in this regression is a scaling factor necessary to adjust the regression for the use of the natural log of civilian nonagricultural employment.

[4] U.S. Bureau of the Census, "Income in 1965 of Families and Persons in the United States," p. 18.

[5] This elasticity is calculated by dividing the regression coefficients by the mean of the percentage of farm families. When the regression is computed with a trend term, the income elasticity drops to zero and the employment elasticity drops to 0.8, but this still leaves the problem of determining what causes the negative trend of 0.3 percentage point per year.

Families outside the Labor Force

Since individuals outside the labor force are attracted into it by the availability of jobs, tight labor markets reduce poverty by reducing the number of families with no one in the labor force.[6] The importance of job opportunities can be seen both over time and across states. After accounting for demographic factors, a rise of 1 percentage point in the number of full-time workers lowers the percentage of families with no one in the labor force by 0.4 percentage point across states, and a decline of 1 percentage point in unemployment reduces the number of families with no earner by 0.2 percentage point over time (see regressions E-3 and E-4).[7]

Across states for 1960 the regression results are:

(E-3) $L = 15.6297 + 0.3277F + 0.4766A - 0.3859W + 16.4915D$

(5.0543) (0.1783) (0.1767) (0.0952) (4.0877)
**   **   **   **

$$\overline{R}^2 = 0.86 \qquad \text{d.f.} = 46 \qquad S_e = 2.7$$

where

L = percentage of families with no one in the labor force
F = percentage of families with female head
A = percentage of families with head over sixty-four
W = percentage of population fourteen years old and over who work 50–52 weeks per year
D = dummy for Alaska and Hawaii.

Note: The standard errors of the coefficients are shown in parentheses.
** Coefficient significant at 0.01 level.

Over time with national data for 1947–63 the regression results are:

(E-4) $L_e = 11.6880 + 0.5716F + 0.9819A + 0.2204U$

(3.4875) (0.1397) (0.3713) (0.0968)
**   **   *   *

$$\overline{R}^2 = 0.80 \qquad \text{d.w.} = 1.51 \qquad \text{d.f.} = 13 \qquad S_e = 0.37$$

[6] Tella, "The Relation of Labor Force to Employment."

[7] Two different economic variables and two slightly different dependent variables must be used, since the percentage of full-time workers and the percentage of families with no one in the labor force are not available annually for the full postwar period. The percentage of families with no one in the labor force differs from the percentage of families with no earner, since the labor force figure refers to a survey week and the earner figure refers to the whole year.

where

L_e = percentage of families with no wage earner

U = unemployment rate.

Note: The standard errors of the coefficients are shown in parentheses.
* Coefficient significant at 0.05 level.
** Coefficient significant at 0.01 level.

A decline of 1 percent in unemployment causes the number of families with no earner to decline by 100,000 families, and a rise of 1 percent in the number of full-time workers causes the number of families with no one in the labor force to decline by 200,000 families. Many families can be enticed into the labor force, but that point should be placed in perspective by the fact that they represent less than 3 percent of the total number of families in each category.[8] The long-run responsiveness to job opportunities would be larger than the short-run responsiveness, but the vast majority of the families now outside the labor force would still be outside it at higher levels of utilization.

[8] Calculated from data in U.S. Bureau of the Census, "Income in 1965 of Families and Persons in the United States."

The Trade-off between Unemployment and Inflation

To make an intelligent choice between the losses from inflation and the losses from unemployment, detailed empirical information must be available on both the actual relations between unemployment and inflation (if any) and on the distribution and magnitude of gains and losses.[1] Even if the aggregate losses from inflation happened to be greater than the losses from unemployment, the income class distribution of losses could lead to decisions to reduce unemployment rather than inflation.

The costs of unemployment are a combination of the actual losses in production due to not fully utilizing every available man and the costs in terms of human dignity (and the associated social problems) when an individual is unable to support himself or his family. The direct economic losses can be estimated by the associated reduction in actual output. Every 1 percentage point on the unemployment rate means the loss of approximately $25 billion per year in GNP. The human costs may be less easily measured, but they may very well be much more important.

The human effects become especially important since unemployment is not evenly distributed throughout the population. If a 4 percent unemployment rate meant that each worker was unemployed 4 percent of the time, unemployment would probably have very few social consequences. If a 4 percent unemployment rate meant that 4 percent of the population was unemployed all of the time, unemployment would probably be an important cause of poverty, delinquency, broken homes, and a host of social ills.

Although neither extreme represents the actual situation, unemploy-

[1] See Chap. 4, p. 65.

ment is very heavily concentrated among the unskilled and minority groups. A national unemployment target of 4 percent seems to imply Negro unemployment of 8 percent. Consideration of the social benefits which would accrue from lower Negro unemployment might very well lead to the goal of a 4 percent unemployment rate among Negroes. Unless other policies can radically alter economic institutions and attitudes, a necessary part of a 4 percent Negro unemployment rate might be a national unemployment target between 2 and 3 percent.

The costs of inflation include lower relative incomes to fixed income recipients. If inflation reaches very high levels and distorts resource allocation decisions, an additional cost may be a lower potential output. The income losses from inflation must be evaluated in terms of the desired income distribution and after all offsetting changes have been considered. Thus, inflation may not lower real standards of living among most fixed income recipients if Social Security payments are escalated to offset the effects of inflation. From the point of view of income distribution, the losses from inflation might be weighted less heavily than the losses from unemployment if they occur among a wealthier group. In any case, the problem cannot be decided theoretically. Calculations must be made in order to compare the empirical gains and losses.

Unemployment is a direct measure of the utilization of the available labor force, but, since it is also an important measure (if not the only measure) of the entire economy's resource utilization, economists have devoted extensive efforts to finding a stable relationship between unemployment and price increases. No one denies that resource utilization affects inflation, but the exact relation between unemployment and price increases is another problem. Reasonable connections have been found between them (the Phillips curve), but in the American economy the relation does not seem to be so precise.

Although a completely acceptable price equation has not been found, price equations do present some interesting information on the connections between inflation and utilization levels. The price equation (F-1) presented here has as the dependent variable either the percentage change in the GNP deflator or the percentage change in the wholesale price index. The independent variables are unit labor costs, unemployment, unemployment squared, and the change in unemployment. The price equations are estimated using annual data from 1929 to 1965, with the observations during the Second World War, the immediate postwar readjustment, and the Korean war eliminated. The years included are 1929–41, 1948–50, and 1953–65.

TABLE F-1

Price Equation Estimates, 1929-65[a]

Dependent variable		Constant term	Unemployment rate U	Unemployment rate squared U^2	Percentage change in unemployment rate ΔU	Percentage change in unit labor costs ΔL	Coefficient of determination $\bar{R}^2$	Durbin-Watson statistic d.w.	Degrees of freedom d.f.	Standard error S_e
Percentage change in GNP deflator	1	4.7701 (1.9267)	−0.6217 (0.3760)	0.0199 (0.1478)	−0.9747 (0.1478)		0.63	2.22	22	2.3
	2	3.0481 (1.2362)	−0.5976 (0.2346)	0.0238 (0.0088)	−0.4613 (0.1262)	0.6079 (0.1171)	0.86	2.57	21	1.4
Percentage change in wholesale price index	3	5.6324 (2.6258)	−1.0688 (0.5125)	0.0420 (0.0191)	−1.8210 (0.2015)		0.75	2.39	22	3.1
	4	3.6377 (2.0425)	−1.0409 (0.3877)	0.0465 (0.0145)	−1.2261 (0.2085)	0.8084 (0.1935)	0.86	2.12	21	2.3

Source: Estimated from equation (F-1). The unit labor cost term, omitted in lines 1 and 3, is included in lines 2 and 4. The standard errors of the coefficients are shown in parentheses.

a. The war and postwar years 1942–47 and 1951–52 are excluded.

(F-1) $$\Delta P = a - bU + cU^2 - d\Delta U + e\Delta L$$

where

$\Delta P =$ percentage change in GNP deflator or percentage change in the wholesale price index

$U =$ national unemployment rate

$\Delta L =$ percentage change in unit labor costs (current dollar employee compensation as a ratio of constant dollar GNP).

For first difference regressions, the results are reasonably good, as shown in Table F-1.

The level of unemployment affects the rate of increase of prices in these equations, but the effect is nonlinear. The higher the level of utilization, the larger the increase in prices. A change in the unemployment level from 5 to 4 percent would raise the rate of increase of the wholesale price index by 0.6 percentage point, but a change from 4 percent to 3 percent would cause another 0.8 percentage point increase. In addition to the nonlinear effect of the level of utilization, the speed of movement also has an important effect. During the year in which unemployment is falling by 1 percentage point, wholesale prices would rise by an additional 1.2 percentage points. After the change had been accomplished, this source of price increases would disappear. Since utilization levels also affect wage increases, further interconnections between utilization and inflation would occur through the unit labor cost term.

The equations also indicate the difficulty of completely stopping inflation by using unemployment as an instrumental variable. If unit labor costs were constant, a 7 percent unemployment rate would be necessary to hold the GNP deflator constant and a 4.4 percent unemployment rate would be necessary to hold wholesale prices constant.

With constant unit labor costs and a 3 percent unemployment rate, there would be an upward trend in wholesale prices of 1.0 percent and of 1.5 percent in the GNP deflator. If unit labor costs rose by 1.7 percent per year (the 1965 rate of increase), wholesale prices would rise by 2.4 percent and the GNP deflator would rise by 2.6 percent per year. In the year in which unemployment was falling from 4 to 3 percent, the upward increases in prices would be 3.6 percent for wholesale prices and 3.1 percent for the GNP deflator. Rates of increase of roughly this magnitude are not fast enough to spiral to ever higher rates or to destroy efficient patterns of resource allocation, but even a slow inflation has some effect on the income distribution.

If we assume that unemployment and inflation are inversely related in the manner indicated, policy makers need to raise or lower desired unemployment targets until the marginal social costs of unemployment and inflation are equal. If the costs of inflation are greater than those of unemployment, the unemployment target should be increased. If the reverse is true, the unemployment target should be decreased.

Although balancing the costs of unemployment and inflation is an unavoidable part of fiscal policy, there are other methods of mitigating the undesirable income losses of the unemployed or those who suffer from inflation. Instruments for redistributing income (principally unemployment insurance and Social Security) can help the victims of either unemployment or inflation, but full compensation can occur only if the government aims for full employment and plans to offset any undesirable effects caused by the concomitant inflation. Unemployment reduces the total output to be divided; inflation does not, unless it reaches to very high levels. Full employment provides the extra resources necessary for redistribution to those who suffer from inflation, but stable prices do not provide the real resources necessary to compensate those who suffer from unemployment.

A program for full employment with an income redistribution policy to offset the effects of inflation could achieve both efficiency (maximum output) and equity (the desired income distribution). If economic policies were flexible enough to accomplish this, however, they would probably be flexible enough to eliminate inflation before full employment was reached. When income redistribution systems cannot be established, the government is faced with the choice of lowering the incomes of those subject to unemployment or of those subject to the effects of inflation. This is a difficult decision but an unavoidable one.

APPENDIX G

The Human Capital Function

To use the human capital function for an analysis of male incomes, equation (5-3) must be estimated in the following form:[1]

$$\text{(G-1)} \quad \ln I = A + b_1 \ln Ed_1 + b_2 \ln Ed_2 + b_3 \ln Ed_3 + c_1 \ln Ex_1$$
$$+ c_2 \ln Ex_2 + c_3 \ln Ex_3 + c_4 \ln Ex_4$$

where

$I =$ mean income level
$Ed_1 =$ years of education to a maximum of 8
$Ed_2 =$ years of education to a maximum of 12
$Ed_3 =$ more than 12 years of education
$Ex_1 =$ years of experience to a maximum of 5
$Ex_2 =$ years of experience to a maximum of 15
$Ex_3 =$ years of experience to a maximum of 35
$Ex_4 =$ more than 35 years of experience.

To calculate the elasticities for different levels of education and experience, the b and c coefficients are added together. Thus the elasticity for the 0–8 years educational range is $b_1 + b_2 + b_3$, the elasticity for the 9–12 years range is $b_2 + b_3$, and the elasticity for the above 12 years range is simply b_3. The elasticities of experience are calculated in a similar manner. Since the log of zero is negative infinity, individuals with no education are inserted at the value of 0.01 year of education rather than at their actual value.

Terminal education and experience ranges were dropped from the regression if they did not exceed their standard errors. In each case there were approximately 65 degrees of freedom. In some cases two or three income cells were blank due to an insufficient number of observations in the cells. Appendix Table G-1 shows the regression results.

[1] See Chap. 5, p. 76.

TABLE G-1

Regression Results for Human Capital Function, Males, 1960

Variable	Constant term A	Elasticities of education			Elasticities of experience				Coefficient of determination $\bar{R}^2$	Standard error S_e
		b_1	b_2	b_3	c_1	c_2	c_3	c_4		
Total white	7.0387 (0.0535)	−0.6129 (0.2131)	−1.0140 (0.4286)	1.7313 (0.2703)	−0.5100 (0.0965)	0.7956 (0.1815)	−0.0859 (0.1136)	0.0	0.89	0.225
Total nonwhite	6.6633 (0.0573)	−0.6839 (0.1919)	−0.5664 (0.3907)	1.3348 (0.2480)	−0.3897 (0.0949)	0.7881 (0.1638)	−0.1378 (0.1015)	0.0	0.89	0.201
North white	7.1536 (0.0515)	−0.4207 (0.2051)	−1.1772 (0.4124)	1.6979 (0.2601)	−0.5017 (0.0929)	0.7600 (0.1746)	−0.0574 (0.1093)	0.0	0.89	0.217
North nonwhite	6.9208 (0.0515)	−0.4533 (0.1725)	−0.7074 (0.3512)	1.2235 (0.2230)	−0.3557 (0.0853)	0.7365 (0.1473)	−0.1089 (0.0913)	0.0	0.89	0.181
South white	6.8557 (0.0561)	−0.7906 (0.2236)	−1.0131 (0.4497)	1.9107 (0.2836)	−0.5501 (0.1013)	0.9592 (0.1904)	−0.2103 (0.1192)	0.0	0.89	0.236
South nonwhite	6.5635 (0.0528)	−0.4908 (0.1768)	−1.1655 (0.3599)	1.7374 (0.2285)	−0.3693 (0.0875)	0.8712 (0.1509)	−0.2598 (0.0935)	0.0	0.89	0.185

Source: Estimated from equation (G-1). See pp. 75–76 for data sources. The standard errors of the coefficients are shown in parentheses.

APPENDIX H

Critique of the Human Capital Function

The human capital function developed in Chapter 5 is not definitive since it ignores many factors that may influence incomes. Creativity, ability, entrepreneurial spirit, and the willingness to undertake risks are all ignored. They are difficult to quantify, but perhaps some method will eventually be found to take them into account. Other points to be noted are the following.

(1) The variables that have been included are not measured in an optimum manner. Ideally, a quality corrected index of education attainment and a quality corrected index of hours of training (formal and informal) would be desirable. Years of education are only a rough measure of the skills imparted by education, and years of experience are certainly a rough measure of the skill imparted on the job.

(2) Using cross-sectional data to evaluate the marginal products of education and experience is subject to the usual objections. Education and experience at different historical periods may be very different. Yet the model assumes that one year of education has the same value regardless of whether acquired in 1920 or 1950. Income levels also rise over time. Consequently, the marginal product of a year of education or experience will rise over time. Additionally, the marginal product of different years of education may not rise proportionally. College education may become more valuable relative to high school education. Most analyses of the returns to education have used cross-sectional data, but this does not eliminate the biases that such data cause.

(3) If conditions are changing rapidly, historical data may provide misleading results. In 1960 the marginal product of a year of college education was smaller for Negroes than for whites. Conditions may have changed enough to make this untrue today. It may be untrue in the future. For purposes of planning, all results need to be tempered by

future expectations. Will the future world resemble the historical world? If it does not, historical human capital functions are relevant only to historical studies and not for future program planning.

(4) Complementarities are built into the human capital function. The human capital function used in Chapter 5 assumes that the elasticity of substitution between education and experience is 1. The results indicate that the explanatory factors should be related to each other in a multiplicative fashion rather than an additive fashion, but the elasticity of substitution may not be 1. The human capital function could easily be extended with constant elasticity of substitution (CES) functions analogous to the CES production functions. The actual elasticity of substitution could be explicitly investigated. Such an investigation is currently under way.

An Incentive System for Upgrading Impoverished Workers

To give Negroes on-the-job experience, as suggested in Chapter 5, either direct grants or tax credits would be given to private firms, nonprofit institutions, state and local governments, or departments of the federal government, based on the amount by which they were able to raise an individual worker's income over a five-year period.

Eligibility Requirements

Any individual whose income is below the maximum covered by the subsidy system would be eligible, with the following exceptions: (1) full-time students; (2) part-time students who do not work full time; (3) those who are within two years of their last year of full-time schooling or within two years of their last year of part-time schooling and part-time work; and (4) individuals over sixty-five years of age.

The first three restrictions are designed to solve the problem of entry into the labor force. Subsidies should not be given to individuals whose incomes are low because they are receiving training or entering the labor market. The two-year requirement should be waived for individuals from families with an income below the poverty line. The program would then have an impact on the problems of poor teen-agers not otherwise possible. Persons over sixty-five are eliminated because training is not the proper answer to their problems.

The program should not be limited to heads of households, but should be open to everyone, since limitation to heads of households will create the same problems as exist in the current welfare system. Such a limitation would encourage male desertion and the creation of female-headed households. To overcome the problem of females who

are returning to work, a two-year work requirement should be insti-
tuted like that for teen-agers. To be eligible for the program, a married
woman must have worked full time in the labor force for two years unless she comes from a family where the family income is below the poverty line. This would allow the program to have an impact on poor females without giving a big subsidy to white middle-class wives who are
returning to work after their children leave home or go to school.

Maximum Income Limits

Subsidies should be provided to encourage increases in income for all
individuals who are now earning less than $4,000. This sum is high
enough to allow the head of a family to lift his family out of poverty,
but is still significantly below the median income for families with a
year-round worker ($9,314 in 1967). Since the amount of subsidy per
dollar of income increase will fall as income rises, the upper limit is not
tremendously important. Most of the subsidy will be given for increases
in income below the $3,000 level.

The Time Path of the Income Stream

Since calculating the increase in income eligible for a subsidy as the
difference in income between the year previous to entry into the program and the fifth year of the program would encourage large income
increases in the fifth year and low incomes in the first four years, the
subsidy must depend on the average income over the five years. It is
still desirable, however, to encourage an upward trend in income, since
most income increases will not be reversible. Thus a weighted average
should be calculated, with the fifth year weighted more heavily than
the first year. I suggest the following set of weights:

Year	Weight
1	0.10
2	0.15
3	0.20
4	0.25
5	0.30

Income in the fifth year would thus be three times as valuable as income in the first year. To prevent firms from playing the system by jug-
gling increases in income into a favorable pattern, there should be a
requirement that the maximum annual increase in income be no
greater than twice the minimum annual increase in income. This will

force income increases to be spread over the period, but will still encourage firms to keep employees for the full five years. Wage payments in later years are more valuable to the firm than wage payments in early years. It is hoped that after five years the workers will be so integrated into the firm that very few will be discharged at the end of the program.

Degree of Progression in the Income Subsidy

Since the utility of increasing very low incomes is presumably greater than the utility of increasing relatively high incomes, a strong degree of progression should be built into the subsidy system.

For the first $1,000, 4 percent of the total subsidy should be given for each $100 increase in incomes; for the second $1,000, 3 percent; for the third $1,000, 2 percent; and for the fourth $1,000, 1 percent.

Thus of the total subsidy 40 percent would go for income increases from $0 to $1,000, 30 percent for increases from $1,000 to $2,000, 20 percent for increases from $2,000 to $3,000, and 10 percent for increases from $3,000 to $4,000. This kind of progression in the income subsidy payment constitutes a bonus to employers as an inducement to reach hard core groups and to make the initial hiring decision.

The Size of the Subsidy

How large a subsidy should be given for raising an individual from an income of zero to a weighted average income of $4,000? If increases in income were constrained so that the maximum annual increase could be no more than twice the minimum annual increase, the smallest amount of income that would create a weighted average of $4,000 over the five-year period is $16,848. The time stream of annual incomes would be the following:

Year	Income
1	$1,053
2	2,106
3	3,159
4	4,212
5	6,318

Although this would be the minimum, most firms would pay considerably more, since it is doubtful that union and labor market restrictions would allow wage adjustments precisely tailored to the subsidy system.

To put the subsidy into perspective, the training costs of current government programs should be observed. Unofficial figures suggest that current Job Corps costs are about $5,000 per man (initially they were much higher) and that total costs under the Manpower Development and Training Act are about $6,500 per man-year of training, with costs per enrollee about $1,600; however, most programs do not last one year. These figures indicate that a rather large subsidy could be given without exceeding the costs of current programs, especially since the costs of the subsidy system are related to actual benefits while the costs of current programs do not necessarily result in any benefits. Thus there are no government risks of failure in the subsidy system. If failure occurs, there are no budgetary costs.

On the basis of these figures, I would suggest $5,000 as the proper subsidy for raising one man's income from $0 to an average of $4,000 over the five-year period. Five thousand dollars is less than one-third of the minimum possible income that can produce the maximum subsidy. In most cases the actual subsidy would be much less, since most individuals do not start at the zero income level. The subsidy could also be adjusted as experience is accumulated.

Potential Costs

To obtain an idea of the maximum cost of such a program, I have calculated the subsidies that must be given over a five-year period if every individual in the labor force were brought up to an income level of $4,000. However, this is an overestimate of the actual costs, since not every individual is eligible and not everyone would be brought up to that level in five years. Based on the 1965 distribution of income, $64 billion would be needed. If a rough correction for program eligibility requirements is made by eliminating teen-agers, the elderly, and women who do not work full time, the costs fall to $40 billion, or $8 billion per year. More precise calculations could be made when and if a specific program has been agreed upon.

Enforcement

The income concept used for enforcement and for calculating the subsidy should be based on the personal income reported on the tax form. Enforcement then would require only a computer check of the income tax files to find income in year zero and the succeeding five years. To be eligible for the program the individual must file an income tax form in year zero, but withholding statements are available for all those who worked during the year.

Training Requirements

No particular training programs should be required of industry or government. Any technique that allows increases in individual incomes would be acceptable. The subsidy would be based solely on ability to increase the incomes of the workers. It is not a subsidy for training labor but for increasing incomes. If this could be done without training or by upgrading other workers and creating vacancies, so much the better.

Special Handicaps

Should the subsidy differ for different groups of individuals, depending on the handicaps they face? Should a black worker with little education and a criminal record receive a larger subsidy than a worker with fewer handicaps? With progression built into the subsidy system, special categories would not need to be established. Workers with the most handicaps have the lowest incomes. The subsidies for increasing incomes would be largest for the lowest income groups. Thus the handicapped could be favored without appearing to discriminate in their favor.

Timing of Payments

The subsidy could be paid in annual installments, with the requirement that the books balance at the end of a five-year period.

Job Mobility

If a worker changed jobs voluntarily, he would be eligible for another five years of subsidies with a new employer, but his initial income would be the last income which he received from the previous employer. Thus the new employer could receive subsidies only to the extent that he is able to raise the worker's income above its level with the previous employer. The old employer, of course, would receive a bonus based on how much he was able to raise the worker's income level. This provision is necessary to prevent immobility in the labor force and create competition for the workers in the program. Private industry risks from job mobility should be covered in the size of the subsidy rather than by preventing job mobility.

If a worker should be fired for not working satisfactorily during the five-year period, no subsidies would be given to the firm. This is a risk which the firm must bear. If a worker was fired because of a slack economy, the firm would be eligible to receive the subsidy coming to it for the time the worker had been employed, if it agreed to rehire the worker at the end of the recession and actually did so.

The Lazy

What should be done about a worker who participates in the program for five years, quits his job, and then enjoys a period of idleness and poverty? Should he be eligible for the program again? I suggest that he be allowed to enter the program again, but not with the same employer. This would prevent sweetheart deals between the employee and the employer.

Depreciated Skills

What should be done about workers who have been earning good incomes but whose skills become obsolete because of technical progress? How long a period of poverty should they be forced to endure before being eligible for the program? One year of low income should be necessary for program eligibility. This would guarantee that skills were really obsolete and that the costs of technical change were not simply being transferred to the federal government. In special cases where large numbers of workers become technologically obsolete, the Secretary of Labor could certify their eligibility.

Conclusions

There are as yet unrealized problems that would emerge during the detailed staff work in trying to design a practical system of income subsidies, but the problems are worth solving.

Methods of Calculating the Distribution of Shift Coefficients, Technical Progress, and Capital-Labor Ratios

Using the actual male human capital functions for whites and Negroes, mean incomes can be calculated for every cell in a matrix of education arrayed against experience, as noted in Chapter 6. Given the actual distributions of individuals across these same matrices, hypothetical distributions of income can be calculated (see Table J-1). They assume that every individual has the same shift coefficient ($783 for nonwhites and $1,140 for whites).

Subtracting the calculated number of persons in each income cell in

TABLE J-1

Actual and Hypothetical Distribution of White Males Eighteen to Sixty-four Years of Age, by Income Class, United States, 1959

(*In thousands*)

Income class	Actual	Hypothetical
$ 0– 1	3,459	216
1– 2	3,610	2,401
2– 3	3,843	3,891
3– 4	4,956	10,968
4– 5	5,943	10,518
5– 6	6,309	7,342
6– 7	4,466	1,040
7–10	5,639	3,992
10–15	2,091	606
15 and over	1,271	0

the hypothetical distribution from the actual number in the same cell provides the number that must be moved into the cell. For example, 215,972 white males were placed in the $0–$1,000 income cell on the basis of education and experience, but 3,458,919 is the actual number in that cell; thus 3,242,947 must be moved into the cell from other cells of the hypothetical income distribution. Since there are only 2,401,486 individuals in the $1,000–$2,000 cell, the remainder must be moved from the $2,000–$3,000 cell.

Assuming that all individuals are located at the midpoint of their income cell, the shift coefficient must be lowered to move some from an income of $1,500 to $500 and others from $2,500 to $500. Working in natural logs to simplify calculations, the ln of $500 is subtracted from the ln of $1,500 to determine the amount by which the shift coefficients (also in lns) must fall. The difference of 1.0986 is thus subtracted from 7.0387. Similarly, the difference between ln $500 and ln $2,500 is subtracted from 7.0987 to provide the shift coefficient for the group moved from $2,500 to $500 incomes. The average shift coefficient for the $0–$1,000 cell is then calculated by taking a weighted average of the individual shift coefficients in the cell.

For the next cell the same procedure is followed, except that this cell now has no hypothetical members since the original individuals in this cell have all been moved into the $0–$1,000 cell; thus 3,610,226 must be moved into the cell from higher cells. Some come from the $2,000–$3,000 cell, but this cell does not contain enough individuals to fill the $1,000–$2,000 cell; thus others must come from the $3,000–$4,000 cell.

At high income levels the procedures are simply reversed. Here there must be additions to the shift coefficients in order to move individuals up in the income distribution. Since capital income becomes important at high income levels, the average wage earnings in the $15,000 and up cell are assumed to be exactly $20,000. Anything above this level is assumed to represent returns to physical capital.

The relations between the shift coefficients of the human capital function and the production function can be seen in equations (J-1), (J-2), and (J-3).[1] Equation (J-1) is the production function transformed into an equation for the marginal product of labor.

$$\text{(J-1)} \qquad \frac{\partial Y}{\partial L(t)} = e^{a+bU} A_1 e^{\alpha t} K_x(t)^{\gamma(1-\lambda)} [(1+z)^t]^{\gamma\lambda} \alpha\lambda L(t)^{\gamma\lambda-1}$$

[1] The variables for these equations are defined in Chap. 5 and App. A.

(J-2) $$\frac{\partial Y}{\partial L(t)} = A_2(t) \prod_{i=1}^{3} Ed_i^b \prod_{k=1}^{4} Ex_k^c$$

(J-3) $$A_2(t) = e^{a+bU} A_1 e^{\alpha t} K_x(t)^{\gamma(1-\lambda)} \alpha \lambda L(t)^{\gamma\lambda-1}.$$

The education and experience portion of the human capital function,

$$\left[\prod_{i=1}^{3} Ed_i^b \prod_{k=1}^{4} Ex_k^c \right],$$

is a substitute for the embodied technical progress in labor variable in the production function $[(1 + z)^t]^{\gamma\lambda}$. Instead of having to assume some constant rate of embodiment in labor, the human capital function allows the calculation of rates of embodiment from changes in the actual distribution of education and experience. Equation (J-2) can be used to evaluate the rate at which increases in education and experience increase the marginal productivity of labor. This rate can be fed into the production function (equation J-1) in place of the embodiment term previously used, but it is very close to the 1 percent per year originally used.

The assumption that half of the necessary difference in the shift coefficient is explained by capital-labor ratios and half by technical progress means that each factor must explain half of the differences in the lns used to calculate shift coefficients. Thus capital-labor ratios must explain 0.54931 of the total drop of 1.09862 in the shift coefficient for the 2,401,486 individuals moved from the $1,000–$2,000 cell into the $0–$1,000 cell.

Assuming that 80 percent of the capital stock is used by males aged eighteen to sixty-four, since they earn approximately 80 percent of total earnings,[2] the average capital-labor ratio was $11,489 in 1959. The log of this is 9.34914. Using the production function results in which the output elasticity with respect to capital was 0.17, capital accounts for 1.58935 of the entire shift coefficient of 7.0387, and technical progress accounts for the remainder of 5.4493.

If capital-labor ratios must explain 0.54931 of the change in the shift coefficient for the 2,401,486 individuals moved into the $0–$1,000 cell from the $1,000–$2,000 cell, the contribution of capital must fall from 1.58935 to 1.04004. This means the capital per worker must be 6.11788 (1.04004/0.17) (in logs) for these 2.4 million individuals instead of the

[2] See Chap. 6, note 5.

average of 9.34914 for the entire population and for the 215,972 individuals who were already in the $0–$1,000 cell. Taking a weighted average of the capital-labor ratios in the cell provides an estimate of the average capital-labor ratio for the cell.

From the production function analysis a 1 percent change in technical progress results in an equivalent increase in the marginal productivity of labor. Thus, if disembodied technical progress must explain 0.54931 of the necessary change in the shift coefficient for the 2,401,486 individuals, the level of technical progress must fall from 5.4493 to 4.9000. Taking antilogs and making the average efficiency level the index base (= 100), the distribution of efficiency levels in Table 6-2 is easily calculated. The same procedure is followed for nonwhites.

To calculate the changes needed to raise all males to the $3,000 income line, take the difference between the ln of $3,000 and the income level in the cell and then calculate the changes in education, capital, or disembodied technical progress necessary to raise those in the lowest income class to $3,000.

APPENDIX K

Bibliographical Notes

Chapter I. The Twin Problems

The classic and still the best introduction to the problems of poverty and discrimination is Gunnar Myrdal, *An American Dilemma*, 2 volumes, Harper & Brothers, 1944, republished in 1962. More recent descriptive studies include: Michael Harrington, *The Other America*, Macmillan, 1962; Herman Miller, *Rich Man, Poor Man*, Thomas Y. Crowell, 1964; Edgar May, *The Wasted Americans*, Harper & Row, 1964; James Morgan and others, *Income and Welfare in the United States*, McGraw-Hill, 1962; Robert M. MacIver (ed.), *Discrimination and National Welfare*, Harper & Brothers, 1949. *Federal Programs for the Development of Human Resources*, A Compendium of Papers Submitted to the Subcommittee on Economic Progress of the U.S. Joint Economic Committee, 90 Cong. 2 sess., 1968, 2 volumes, contains a broad selection of recent writings.

Conceptually, the social welfare function should determine the optimum distribution of income, but welfare economics has generally been able to say very little about it. The best survey of welfare economics is E. J. Mishan, "A Survey of Welfare Economics, 1939–59," *Surveys of Economic Theory*, prepared for the American Economic Association and the Royal Economic Society, Vol. 1: *Money, Interest, and Welfare*, Macmillan and St. Martin's Press, 1965; this article contains an exhaustive bibliography. Classics in the area include: A. C. Pigou, *The Economics of Welfare*, Macmillan, 1952; P. A. Samuelson, *Foundations of Economic Analysis*, Harvard University Press, 1955; J. Graaff, *Theoretical Welfare Economics*, Cambridge University Press, 1957; I. M. D. Little, *A Critique of Welfare Economics*, Oxford University Press, 1950. The possibilities of obtaining a desired income distribution through democratic procedures are analyzed in Kenneth J. Arrow, *Social Choice and Individual Values,* Wiley, 1951. Franklin M. Fisher, "Income Distribution, Value Judgments, and Welfare," *Quarterly Journal of Economics,* 1956, specifically treats the problem of welfare and the income distribution. Kelvin Lancaster and R. G. Lipsey, "The General Theory of Second Best," *Review of Economic Studies,* 1956–57, is the classic description of what happens to welfare economics if the optimum income distribution does not exist.

Good general books on econometrics include: Edmond Malinvaud, *Statistical Methods of Econometrics,* Rand McNally, 1966, which includes an excellent bibliography; John Johnston, *Econometric Methods,* McGraw-Hill, 1963; Arthur Stanley Goldberger, *Econometric Theory,* Wiley, 1964.

Chapter II.   Income as Measurement

The basic data on the American income distribution can be found in Herman P. Miller, *Income Distribution in the United States,* U.S. Bureau of the Census, 1966; T. Paul Schultz, *The Distribution of Personal Income: A Study of Statistics on the Size Distribution of Personal Income in the United States,* Joint Economic Committee, 88 Cong. 2 sess., 1965; and U.S. Bureau of the Census, *Current Population Reports, Consumer Income,* Series P-60, various years.

The basic work on measuring poverty was done by the Council of Economic Advisers in the *Economic Report of the President, January 1964,* and by Mollie Orshansky in five articles in the *Social Security Bulletin:* "Children of the Poor," July 1963; "Counting the Poor: Another Look at the Poverty Profile," January 1965; "Who's Who Among the Poor: A Demographic View of Poverty," July 1965; "Recounting the Poor—A Five-Year Review," April 1966; and "More about the Poor in 1964," May 1966. For a critical review of poverty definitions, see Rose D. Friedman, *Poverty: Definition and Perspective,* American Enterprise Institute for Public Policy Research, 1965.

The classic work on discrimination is Gary S. Becker, *The Economics of Discrimination,* University of Chicago Press, 1957; in his view, discrimination is not measured by income differentials. Victor R. Fuchs, *Differentials in Hourly Earnings by Region and City Size, 1959,* National Bureau of Economic Research, 1967, attempts to estimate earnings differentials after adjusting for differences in labor force quality. The *Report of the National Advisory Commission on Civil Disor-*

ders, Government Printing Office, 1968, gives a variety of recent data on white-Negro differentials. *Negroes in the United States, Their Economic and Social Situation,* U.S. Bureau of Labor Statistics, Bulletin 1511, 1966, contains exhaustive social statistics on these differentials. *Document and Reference Text: An Index to Minority Group Employment Information,* prepared by the Institute of Labor and Industrial Relations, University of Michigan-Wayne State University, under contract with the Equal Employment Opportunity Commission, 1967, presents a voluminous bibliography.

Chapter III. The Causes of Poverty

For regression analysis of time series data on the incidence of poverty, see Lowell E. Gallaway, "The Foundations of the 'War on Poverty,'" *American Economic Review,* March 1965, and Henry Aaron, "The Foundations of the 'War on Poverty' Reexamined," *American Economic Review,* December 1967. Analytic approaches are applied to the incidence of poverty in Alan Batchelder, "Decline in the Relative Income of Negro Men," and W. H. Locke Anderson, "Trickling Down: The Relationship between Economic Growth and the Extent of Poverty among American Families," both in *Quarterly Journal of Economics,* November 1964.

Three articles and comments on the economics of poverty are included in the *American Economic Review,* May 1965: Theodore W. Schultz, "Investing in Poor People; An Economist's View"; Robert J. Lampman, "Approaches to the Reduction of Poverty"; and Alan Batchelder, "Poverty: the Special Case of the Negro."

For a recent discussion of the state of production function theory and analysis, see Murray Brown (ed.), *The Theory and Empirical Analysis of Production,* National Bureau of Economic Research, 1967. The original interest in production functions was started by Charles W. Cobb and P. H. Douglas, "A Theory of Production," *American Economic Review,* March 1928. Recent advances have depended heavily on the work of Robert M. Solow: "Technical Change and the Aggregate Production Function," *Review of Economics and Statistics,* August 1957; "Investment and Technical Progress," in Kenneth J. Arrow, Samuel Karlin, and Patrick Suppes (eds.), *Mathematical Methods in the Social Sciences,* Stanford University Press, 1960; "Technical Progress, Capital Formation, and Economic Growth," *American Economic Review,* May 1962.

Chapter IV.   Aggregate Economic Policies

The foundations of macroeconomic theory are in John Maynard
Keynes, *The General Theory of Employment, Interest and Money*,
Macmillan, 1936. Elementary texts include Charles L. Schultze, *National Income Analysis*, Prentice-Hall, 1964, and Paul A. Samuelson,
Economics, An Introductory Analysis, McGraw-Hill, 1955. A more advanced text is Gardner Ackley, *Macroeconomic Theory*, Macmillan,
1961.

Employment functions have been estimated for most econometric
forecasting models of the American economy. The most elaborate discussion is by Edwin Kuh, "Income Distribution and Employment Over
the Business Cycle," James S. Duesenberry and others (eds.), *The
Brookings Quarterly Econometric Model of the United States*, Rand
McNally, 1965. For a more micro approach to employment decisions,
see Charles C. Holt and others, *Planning Production, Inventories and
Work Force*, Prentice-Hall, 1960. In Lester C. Thurow, "The Changing Structure of Unemployment: An Econometric Study," *Review of
Economics and Statistics*, May 1965, the employment functions are
more disaggregated and related to output rather than the employment
of the preferred group. The *Document and Reference Text* of the
Equal Employment Opportunity Commission, cited in notes for Chapter 2, lists fifteen pages of references on employment of minority groups.

Recent interest in price equations started with A. W. Phillips, "The
Relation Between Unemployment and the Rate of Change of Money
Wage Rates in the United Kingdom, 1861–1957," *Economica*, November 1958. A good critique of the Phillips approach is found in Richard
G. Lipsey, "The Relation between Unemployment and the Rate of
Change of Money Wage Rates in the United Kingdom, 1863–1957: A
Further Analysis," *Economica*, February 1960. The most widely used
wage equations are by George L. Perry, *Unemployment, Money Wage
Rates, and Inflation*, Massachusetts Institute of Technology Press, 1966,
and by Otto Eckstein and Thomas A. Wilson, "The Determination of
Money Wages in American Industry," *Quarterly Journal of Economics*,
August 1962. General price equations can be found in all of the major
econometric forecasting models. The most extensive discussion is by
Charles L. Schultze and Joseph L. Tryon, "Prices and Wages," *The
Brookings Quarterly Econometric Model of the United States*, cited
above.

For general discussions of postwar fiscal policies and their effects on employment see: Wilfred Lewis, Jr., *Federal Fiscal Policy in the Postwar Recessions*, Brookings Institution, 1962; Arthur M. Okun, *The Battle Against Unemployment*, Norton, 1965; Lester C. Thurow (ed.), *American Fiscal Policy*, Prentice-Hall, 1967; and Seymour L. Wolfbein, *Employment, Unemployment and Public Policy*, Random House, 1965.

Chapter V.   Human Capital

There is a very large literature on the impact of education on incomes. The basic work is by Gary S. Becker, *Human Capital*, National Bureau of Economic Research, 1964. Much of the impetus for economic interest in human capital came from Theodore W. Schultz, "Investment in Human Capital," *American Economic Review*, March 1961. Another overall view is presented by Burton A. Weisbrod, "Investing in Human Capital," *Journal of Human Resources*, Summer 1966. Rates of return on education have been widely calculated. The most extensive attempt to adjust for factors other than education is Giora Hanoch, "An Economic Analysis of Earnings and Schooling," *Journal of Human Resources*, Summer 1967. The same issue contains a symposium on rates of return to investment in education. Other calculations of returns to education include: Gary S. Becker and Barry R. Chiswick, "Education and the Distribution of Earnings," *American Economic Review*, May 1966; Eugene Smolensky, "Investment in the Education of the Poor: A Pessimistic Report," *American Economic Review*, May 1966; Finis Welch, "Measurement of the Quality of Schooling," *American Economic Review*, May 1966; H. S. Houthakker, "Education and Income," *Review of Economics and Statistics*, February 1959. For a comparison of the effects of education on different minority groups see Walter Fogel, "The Effect of Low Educational Attainment on Incomes: A Comparative Study of Selected Ethnic Groups," *Journal of Human Resources*, Fall 1966. Illustrative calculations by occupations are given in W. Lee Hansen, "The Economics of Scientific and Engineering Manpower," *Journal of Human Resources*, Spring 1967.

Current controversies about the impact of education on minority groups are covered in James S. Coleman, *Equality of Educational Opportunity*, U.S. Department of Health, Education, and Welfare, 1966. A critique of this report can be found in Samuel Bowles and Henry M. Levin, "The Determinants of Scholastic Achievement—An Appraisal of Some Recent Evidence," *Journal of Human Resources*, Winter 1968.

Information on public and private manpower programs is provided in the annual *Manpower Report of the President,* U.S. Department of Labor, and the *Handbook of Labor Statistics, 1967,* U.S. Department of Labor. The entire Spring 1967 issue of the *Journal of Human Resources* is devoted to a symposium on manpower theory. The *Document and Reference Text* of the Equal Employment Opportunity Commission, cited in the notes for Chapter 2, contains an exhaustive bibliography of reports on manpower programs that affect minority groups. For good discussion of the Negro and manpower programs see: F. Ray Marshall, *The Negro Worker,* Random House, 1967; F. Ray Marshall and Vernon M. Briggs, *The Negro and Apprenticeship,* Johns Hopkins University Press, 1967; and Sterling D. Spero and Abram L. Harris, *The Black Worker: The Negro and the Labor Movement,* Kennikat Press, 1966. Discussions of the interactions between education and manpower programs are found in William F. Brazziel, "Effects of General Education in Manpower Programs," *Journal of Human Resources,* Summer 1966; Thomas H. Patten, Jr., and Gerald E. Clark, Jr., "Literacy Training and Job Placement of Hard-Core Unemployed Negroes in Detroit," *Journal of Human Resources,* Winter 1968. Virtually the only general analysis of on-the-job training is Jacob Mincer, "On-the-Job Training: Costs, Returns, and Some Implications," *Journal of Political Economy,* October 1962, Supplement.

Chapter VI.   The Dispersion of Income

Most of the classic articles on the theory of income distribution, as well as a long bibliography, are found in William Fellner and Bernard F. Haley (eds.), *Readings in the Theory of Income Distribution,* Richard D. Irwin for the American Economic Association, 1951. This volume contains thirty-two articles on different aspects of the income distribution; most of them are oriented to the traditional discussion about the shares of capital and labor. The importance of mobility is stressed in "The Returns to Geographic Mobility: A Symposium," *Journal of Human Resources,* Fall 1967. Economic aspects of risk and uncertainty are covered in R. Duncan Luce and Howard Raiffa, *Games and Decisions,* Wiley, 1957, and J. W. Pratt, Howard Raiffa, and Robert Schlaifer, *Introduction to Statistical Decision,* McGraw-Hill, 1965. The best introduction to the economics of technical progress and capital-labor ratios is found in W. E. G. Salter, *Productivity and Technical Change,* Cambridge University Press, 1960; this book explicitly examines the impact of dispersion on the level of technical progress and capital-labor ratios. The classic book on the theory of monopoly is Edward H. Chamberlin, *The Theory of Monopolistic Competition*, Harvard University Press, 1933 (8th ed., 1962), which contains an exhaustive bibliography. For a discussion of how economic theory must be reformulated with disequilibrium, see Kelvin Lancaster and R. G. Lipsey, "The General Theory of Second Best," cited in the notes for Chapter 1. The distribution of wealth is discussed by Simon Kuznets in *Shares of Upper Income Groups in Income and Savings*, National Bureau of Economic Research, 1953. Gabriel Kolko, *Wealth and Power in America: An Analysis of Social Class and Income Distribution*, Praeger, 1962, examines the implication of dispersions in the ownership of wealth. The distribution of ability and its impact are discussed in most of the articles and books on human capital listed under Chapter 5.

Chapter VII.   Discrimination

Most of the previous work on the theory of discrimination is set out in Gary S. Becker, *The Economics of Discrimination*, University of Chicago Press, 1957, and in Anne O. Krueger, "The Economics of Discrimination," *Journal of Political Economy*, October 1963. The relevant aspects of international trade theory are taxonomically covered in James Edward Meade, *The Theory of International Economic Policy*, 3 volumes, Oxford University Press, 1951. The conditions for retaliation are outlined in Harry G. Johnson, *International Trade and Economic Growth*, George Allen & Unwin, 1958. The monopolistic approach to economic actions is best covered in Edward Chamberlin, *The Theory of Monopolistic Competition*, cited in the notes for Chapter 6.

For empirical work on the impact of economic discrimination, see: Harry J. Gilman, "Economic Discrimination and Unemployment," *American Economic Review*, December 1965; Norval D. Glenn, "Occupational Benefits to Whites from the Subordination of Negroes," *American Sociological Review*, June 1963; Phyllis Groom, "Prices in Poor Neighborhoods," *Monthly Labor Review*, October 1966; Stanley Lieberson and Glenn V. Fuguitt, "Negro-White Occupational Differences in the Absence of Discrimination," *American Journal of Sociology*, September 1967; Paul M. Siegel, "On the Cost of Being a Negro," *Sociological Inquiry*, Winter 1965; David Caplovitz, *The Poor Pay More: Consumer Practices of Low-Income Families*, Free Press of Glencoe, 1963; Victor R. Fuchs, *Differentials in Hourly Earnings by Region and City*

Size, 1959, National Bureau of Economic Research, 1967. An alternative calculation of the economic costs of discrimination is given in the *Economic Report of the President, January 1965.* Myrdal, *An American Dilemma,* cited in the notes for Chapter 1, probably still contains the best description of the impact of discrimination.

Chapter VIII.   Limitations and Alternatives

Christopher Green, in *Negative Taxes and the Poverty Problem,* Brookings Institution, 1967, sets out the problem of income maintenance and discusses the advantages and disadvantages of the negative income tax in detail; the book also contains a good bibliography. Some alternative methods of income maintenance, such as Social Security, unemployment compensation, and public assistance, are discussed in Otto Eckstein (ed.), *Studies in the Economics of Income Maintenance,* Brookings Institution, 1967. A detailed appraisal of the Social Security System is carried out in Joseph A. Pechman, Henry J. Aaron, and Michael K. Taussig, *Social Security: Perspectives for Reform,* Brookings Institution, 1968.

Other studies of the negative income tax include: Milton Friedman, "Poverty: A Direct Approach," *Context,* Winter 1964; Lowell E. Gallaway, "Negative Income Tax Rates and the Elimination of Poverty," *National Tax Journal,* September 1966; George H. Hildebrand, "Second Thoughts on the Negative Income Tax," *Industrial Relations,* February 1967; Michael D. Reagan, "Washington Should Pay Taxes to the Poor," *New York Times Magazine,* February 20, 1966; James Tobin, "On Improving the Economic Status of the Negro," *Dædalus,* Fall 1965; and James Tobin, Joseph A. Pechman, and Peter M. Mieszkowski, "Is a Negative Income Tax Practical?" *Yale Law Journal,* November 1967, Brookings Reprint 142. An alternative approach is set out in Robert Theobald, *The Guaranteed Income: Next Step in Economic Evolution?* Doubleday, 1966.

The guaranteed job approach to income maintenance was first officially proposed by the report of the National Commission on Technology, Automation, and Economic Progress in *Technology and the American Economy,* Government Printing Office, 1966. A recent economic study of public assistance is C. T. Brehm and T. R. Saving, "The Demand for General Assistance Payments," *American Economic Review,* December 1964. The National Commission on Income Maintenance is currently preparing a report.

INDEX

Index

Ability. *See* Intelligence
Aged: direct income transfer for, 149; families headed by, 141–42, 143
Alaska, 42–43
Anderson, W. H. Locke, 61*n*
Arrow, Kenneth, 163*n*

Bargaining power of labor, 107–08
Becker, Gary S., 87*n*, 88, 112, 113, 116, 117, 124, 129
Bowles, Samuel, 38*n*
Brady, Dorothy S., 15*n*

Capital (physical): comparison with human capital, 84*n*; growth of, and marginal productivity of labor, 28, 29; interdependence with human capital, 71; labor as substitute for, 47*n*, 92; Negro access to, 123–24; returns to, by increasing skill of workers, 86–87; supply of, 120
Capital-labor ratios: distribution of, 199–200; effect of, on dispersion of income, 97, 102–07
CEA. *See* Council of Economic Advisers
Costs: of eliminating discrimination, 135–37; of subsidy program, 194; of training, 87–88
Council of Economic Advisers (CEA), 22, 23, 109

Denison, Edward F., 26*n*, 28*n*, 167
Discrimination: in access to capital, 123–24; Becker theory of, 112–16; definition of, 112; economic effects of eliminating, 134–37; in employment, 118–19, 130–31, 135; government role in, 127, 129–30; in housing, 122, 125, 127–28; in human capital investment, 122–23, 132; inefficiency losses from, 121–22; monopoly power as cause of, 124, 133, 138; Negro losses from, 133–34; in occupation, 121–22, 124, 128–29, 132–33; in prices, 123, 125; social benefits from eliminating, 137–38; social pressures to enforce, 127–28; social versus physical distance in, 117; in wages, 119–21, 122–23, 126, 131–32; white economic gains from, 133–34. *See also* Negroes

Economic growth, sources of, 26–27, 166–68
Education: of adults, 45, 95; effects of, for Negroes versus whites, 77–80; equalizing levels of, 136–37; experience and, 74, 76–78, 94–95, 189; human capital and, 67–70; incidence of poverty and, 37–39; income distribution and, 66–67, 76–78; results of, in North versus

211